A transplanted Washingtonian, MAXINE KNOX *thinks of herself as a retired executive secretary and a tired mother of four sons. For five years she also edited a house organ for a large food manufacturing concern. Since moving to the Monterey Peninsula, Maxine has turned to writing newspaper advertising and radio commercials and doing business promotion for hotels and restaurants. The Knox family has lived in Pacific Grove for many years.*

As the wife of a Navy Commander, MARY RODRIGUEZ *lived in many places, but when the time came for her husband to retire, the Rodriguez family, including three daughters, chose Monterey as their permanent home. Mary has worked for the Springfield Ohio News-Sun, Honolulu Star-Bulletin and now is a staff writer for the Monterey Peninsula Herald. Her stories have appeared in all leading children's magazines. She has also written a juvenile book, "Hawaiian Spelling Bee."*

A mutual hobby, contesting, brought Maxine and Mary together fifteen years ago, and their warm friendship grew into a writing team. Together they wrote the "Monterey Peninsula Travel Guide" for the Monterey Peninsula Visitors and Convention Bureau in 1972. This book is their second team effort.

BY MAXINE KNOX
AND MARY RODRIGUEZ
WARD RITCHIE PRESS · LOS ANGELES

EXPLORING BIG SUR
MONTEREY · CARMEL

Highway One Country

This book is
fondly dedicated to
Ted Krough,
our "middle man"

The material in this book is reviewed and updated
at each printing.

Cover color photo courtesy Ernest Beyl
Title page art by Roy Nickerson

CONTENTS

Exploring the highways and byways of Big Sur and the Monterey Peninsula has given us a deeper appreciation for the area in which we live, has strengthened old friendships and garnered new friends. The information in this book could not have been gathered without the help of old-time residents who supplied background material and newcomers who still view the Monterey Peninsula through visitors' eyes. We thank them all. We are especially grateful to the Monterey Peninsula, Pacific Grove, Seaside and Moss Landing Chambers of Commerce; Monterey Peninsula Herald; Carmel Pine Cone; Key Magazine; Hobbit Mines; Del Monte Properties Company; Group 4 Advertising; Carmel Business Association; Artichoke Industries, Inc. and California Artichoke and Vegetable Growers Corporation.

INTRODUCTION

The Big Sur/Monterey Peninsula area has a special magic all its own—rocky coastline, white sandy beaches, primeval forests, mist-shrouded mountains, crisp smog-free air and an historic and artistic atmosphere—all of which will make you want to return again and again. Each time you will discover something new and different to do and to see. You can enjoy a restful holiday or a visit crammed with challenging activities and adventures because there is something for everyone of every age and every interest:

Hike into an unspoiled natural wilderness and fish in a quiet mountain stream.

Spend a day on an Italian fishing boat and bring back a big one.

Follow the blazed trails of Father Serra and Soldier Portola and delve into California's colorful history.

Return to the nostalgic setting of Steinbeck's "Cannery Row."

Stand in awe when you actually see the Lone Cypress, familiar to you only in pictures heretofore.

Watch playful otters cracking mussels in the kelp beds or seals panhandling from a captivated audience or migrating gray whales making their way along the Coast.

Browse through fabled shops and countless galleries and artists' studios in Carmel-by-the-Sea.

Golf on a championship course in "the golf capital of the world" or play tennis on a choice of fine courts.

Enjoy a perfect dinner in a candlelit, firelit restaurant overlooking seascape and treescape.

Or how about just relaxing on a wide, white sandy ocean beach?

Jutting out into the blue Pacific, the Monterey Peninsula is framed by the rolling ocean on two sides and the lulling waters of Monterey Bay on the other, with the forest greenery and majestic mountains of Big Sur completing the canvas. Located on the Central California Coast, it is 125 miles south of San Francisco and 345 miles north of Los Angeles and is easily accessible by car, bus or plane. Running through the Monterey Peninsula and connecting with major highways to the north, south and east is California's first designated Scenic Highway, Highway 1 through the Big Sur country. Greyhound Bus Lines, an intra-city bus service with friendly, helpful drivers and charter bus tours are provided. Three scheduled airlines service the Peninsula, and private plane facilities are excellent.

The climate is pleasantly temperate. In the winter months, when rainy days alternate with sun-filled weeks, the average temperature is 57°. The average high summer temperature is 67°. Morning and evening fogs cool the coastline in the summertime but generally disappear by mid-morning. It is never really cold and seldom hot, nearly always sweater-weather. You can golf or fish during any month. Casual clothes are acceptable almost everywhere.

Because the Monterey Peninsula is so attractive to visitors and a popular choice for large conferences and small group meetings, it is well to plan ahead so you won't be confronted by "no vacancy" signs. This is particularly true in the summer months and also during the time of special annual events, such as the Bing Crosby National Pro-Am Golf Tournament, Laguna Seca Races and the Monterey Jazz Festival. For an uncrowded holiday, consider the fall and winter months when some motels have lower rates, and check the listing of Extraspecial Events in the last chapter of this book. If you decide to attend one of these exciting happenings, reserve your tickets, if needed, and your accommodations well ahead of time.

The Monterey Peninsula is made up of several individualized communities: Monterey, Pacific Grove, Pebble Beach, Carmel, Carmel Valley, Seaside and Marina. Though of divergent origins, they complement each other and merge into a delightful area different from anywhere you have ever been. By taking you along a simple route, this book will help you discover the special magic of Big Sur and the Monterey Peninsula on your own.

Point Sur beacon lights the night.

I EXPLORING BIG SUR

Big Sur is the name given to the ruggedly beautiful seacoast country stretching north from the Monterey County line to the Carmel River. This now-famous coast route is one of the world's most spectacular highways. Seventy-two scenic miles connect Southern California with the Monterey Peninsula. The highway was built at a cost of ten million dollars, took sixteen years to build and was opened in 1937. It was planned to take advantage of the breathtaking views as it hugs the natural rocky-coved shoreline, twists along steep cliffs, spans canyons formed by rushing rivers and ambles along foam-fringed ocean beaches. At some places the road ascends almost a thousand feet above sea level, then sweeps grandly around a point and descends to within fifty feet of a comely cove. The dramatic contrast between the restless, sometimes vehement sea and the serene beauty of primitive forests and magnificent mountains is unforgettable. Big Sur is an oasis in a day when wilderness is fast disappearing. Prior to the opening of Highway 1, it took half a day over a narrow unsafe road through dense thicket and virgin timber to get to Monterey from Big Sur. Prior to that there was only a horse trail for hauling supplies to the few inhabitants along the coast.

The Indians were called "Costanoans" or "coast people." Years before the white settlers came, the Esselens in the Big Sur area hunted sea lions but lived mainly on a diet of fish and shellfish, supplemented with nuts, berries and roots, and seasoned with seaweed.

John B. R. Cooper, who took the name "Juan Bautista Cooper" when he adopted Mexican citizenship, was a shrewd trader. He accumulated much wealth and land, including Rancho El Sur, where he and his family lived when they were not in Monterey. The Big Sur country took its name from this rancho.

More species of birds are found in this coastal area than anywhere else in California. Many animals, from mice to mountain lions, thrive in its forests. The phantom white orchid grows high in the mysterious canyons, while rare ferns and wildflowers lace the inland streams.

The best time to drive Highway 1 is between noon and 6:00 p.m. when the inspiring views are not shrouded in coastal fog. Be alert if you are at the wheel; this road changes with the turns, the hours, the days and the seasons. Make sure you have film in your camera, take your time and linger to admire and enjoy this unduplicated seacoast called Big Sur. It's full of big surprises!

Salmon Creek waterfall, a few miles north of the Monterey County line, is in the southernmost stand of sequoia redwoods. This is also an important steelhead trout spawning area. From the first heavy rains in the fall through January, steelhead spawn in most of the large creeks to the north, also.

Just before you reach tiny Gorda, the last stop on the Big Sur mail run, a narrow dirt road leads up to the Los Burros Mining District. The mining roads are steep, rough, dusty, dry and dangerous; a four-wheel drive vehicle is needed. The District stretches from San Carpoforo Creek north to Plaskett Ridge. Most of the land east of Hunter Liggett Military Reservation is open to prospecting and mining exploration, except that which is currently being privately worked for valuable minerals. Do not explore, prospect, hunt or fish on land that may be inhabited. Mining claims may not be clearly marked, but trespassing is met sternly.

After leaving the Mother Lode, a few Chinese began exploring along the creeks in Jolon Valley. They found a little gold, continued west and eventually returned to their ancestral occupation of fishing. Around 1855 gold-bearing gravels were found in the westerly Santa Lucia Mountains, and many more miners moved in. The Los Burros Mining District was formed by these miners in the 1870's. The District still produces small amounts of gold, silver, chromium, jade and quicksilver. Every element known in the earth's crust and almost every geological condition is found in a small way somewhere in these high mountains. Even platinum has been found in the streams. A few present-day prospectors are seeking the legendary "pot of gold." They work the old mines and skillfully recover tiny amounts of precious metals or hunt for large jade deposits near the coast.

Jade Cove has produced perhaps a million dollars' worth of quality nephrite jade in rare blue-green colors. The fine Pacific Blue Jade, found nowhere else in the world, is worth over two hundred dollars a pound. Prize specimens of this color are sought by collectors world over. In 1971 a five-ton piece of jade, eight feet long, was pried from a ledge near Jade Cove after six months of hard labor. It is believed to be the largest piece of jade ever found in North America. Rockhounds have been busy for many years, but it is still possible to find small pieces of jade on the beach and in the serpentine cliffs at this cove. Skindivers can bring up larger pieces. Most jade collected nowadays is the common green and black serpentine and far from the real thing. The best specimens are found at low tide or after a winter storm.

It is easier to get down to Jade Cove beach at Willow Creek. There is a picnic area at Plaskett Creek, just south of Willow Creek, with trailer and camping facilities, and the same at Sand Dollar Picnic Area at the north end of Jade Cove. Both are U.S. Forest Service Campgrounds.

Long-time Big Sur residents, Janet and Edward Jones, discovered the end of their rainbow deep in the Santa Lucia Mountains in 1966 and founded Hobbit Mines. Their studio is at the mine and not open to the public because of inaccessibility. It is typical of the craft guilds throughout the Monterey Peninsula area that create a wide range of practical works of art. Hobbit Mines is a cottage industry of local designer-craftsmen who make quality hand-wrought gemstone artifacts. They mine and cut jade, hand-polish gemstones from around the world and set them in gold or silver. In addition to local gems, opals, lapis lazuli, emeralds and rubies are mounted in settings patterned after the distinctive provincial art of the Etruscan era. Their jewelry, called "Canyon Originals," is sold at the Phoenix, Highlands Inn and in better shops throughout the Peninsula. Hobbit Mines will also assess your local jade finds.

Pacific Valley is bordered by Prewitt Creek on the south and Wild Cattle Creek on the north. This is a four-mile stretch of rather level road before the curves and heights. Access to the beach is easy for surf-fishermen and skindivers.

From the south end of Kirk Creek Bridge, Nacimiento Grade winds and climbs to nearly 4,000 feet and then down to Jolon Valley, about thirty miles. This is not an easy road to drive. The highway leading out of Jolon, which is much better, goes to King City (20 miles) on U.S. Highway 101. The Portola expedition camped in Jolon Valley in 1769, and in 1771 Father Junipero Serra founded the third California Mission here, San Antonio de Padua, which eventually became one of the richest and most populous of the chain as hundreds of Indians were converted. Jolon became a very active station on the wagon road between San Francisco and Los Angeles. A water-power flour mill, now restored, was built in 1806 to grind the grain for which the Valley was famous. The State began restoration of the Mission in 1903, but the work was ruined by the 1906 earthquake. With the help of a grant from the William Randolph Hearst Foundation in 1948, San Antonio Mission was restored. At the outbreak of World War II, the Federal Government purchased thousands of acres of land from Hearst to establish Hunter Liggett Military Reservation. Headquarters are at Hearst's former hunting lodge, which

14

looks like another mission. Permits for fishing and hunting on the reservation may be purchased at their wildlife office. If you are seeking hot weather, you'll find it in oak-dotted Jolon Valley in the summertime.

Limekiln Creek Bridge spans a beautiful natural canyon with a waterfall. In the mid-1800's schooners picked up bricks from the limekilns operating at the mouth of the creek, which are still intact along its edge. Jasper and iron pyrite can be found and occasionally agates and garnets, but not very good ones. For a time there was a hippie commune here, but Limekiln Beach Redwoods Campground is now privately owned and is open year-round. It has a freshwater pool and trout stream, ocean beach, and trails to the old limekilns.

There are good campsites, trailer spaces and a picnic area overlooking the ocean, plus modern restrooms, at Kirk Creek Campground, operated by the U.S. Forest Service.

The Benedictine Order was founded in the 11th century in the Appenines near Florence, Italy, a setting much like that of the New Camaldoli and its Immaculate Heart Heritage. This is the only American branch of the Order and was established in 1958 on the former Lucia Ranch, 1,300 feet above sea level in the Santa Lucia Mountains. The gentle Camaldolese monks are dedicated to a hermit-like life of prayer and creative and scholarly duties. Visitors are allowed in the guest house. The anteroom is a little shop with religious artifacts and books, plus carvings and artworks made by the monks. Delicious brandied fruitcake is made in the Hermitage kitchen year-round and is sold here and in The Hermitage Shop in Carmel. The public rarely sees any of the forty some resident monks. Women are admitted only to the guest house and church.

From Little Lucia and Lopez Point the highway curls north toward Partington Ridge, which you can see in the distance, and a waterfall tumbling down from the mountainside.

A sylvan setting along the old coast road.

At least 700 years ago the Esselen Indians probably watched Cabrillo and Vizcaino making their way up the coast to explore California. Diggings have shown that an Indian village with a population of about 100 flourished near Big Creek Bridge. The total Esselen (variously spelled) population along the coast was around 500. The area is all private property now.

John Little State Reserve (21 acres) at Lime Creek has no facilities as yet but is open to the public for daytime use only. Fog hangs over this spot in the summertime. When clear, however, the view of the coast is tremendous.

Located at Old Slate's Hot Springs overlooking the ocean is Esalen Institute, now known nation-wide for its programs to expand human potential. The sign at the front gate reads "By Reservation Only," which, loosely translated, probably means "Keep Out."

California State law made prisoners available for highway work on a paid basis. Some of the convicts who helped build Highway 1 lived in shacks near Anderson Creek and Kirk Creek. From here work proceeded in two directions. Later it became an art colony. In the mid-forties Henry Miller, famed author, and Emil White, painter of primitives, lived here.

Only the parking and picnic areas and trail to the headland are open to the public at Julia Pfeiffer Burns State Park (1,725 acres). There is a steep path leading to a small beach at the mouth of the creek, another path to the old tanbark dock, and it is only a short walk to a spot overlooking the waterfall where McWay Creek plummets fifty feet into the ocean.

The cluster of small mailboxes on the road belong to the families living atop Partington Ridge. In November you can sit on the wooden bench on the oceanside and watch California gray whales migrating to their breeding and calving areas in Lower California and see them return in the spring to their feeding grounds in the Bering Sea, an 11,000-mile journey. These huge mammals are thirty to fifty feet long and weigh about a ton a foot.

Jaimie de Angulo, who lived on the Ridge, shared the beauties of his land in death as he did in life. De Angulo Trail was donated to the U.S. Forest Service and leads to the top of Partington Ridge for a great view of the raw coastline. It is three miles to the Coast Ridge Road, four miles to Cold Springs Camp and nine miles to the south fork of the Big Sur River. This is a mountainous trail and should be climbed by experienced hikers only.

Drive carefully over Torre Canyon Bridge; the curves are sharp. The Coast Gallery at the north end of the bridge beside the stream of Lafler Canyon is the historic center and showplace for Big Sur artists and craftsmen and also features sculptured sandcast candles by "K the Candler" and books by local authors.

If it is safe to do so, cross over and park on the oceanside across from Grimes Canyon. You will hear the barking of a huge herd of seals 700 feet below. This is a sheer drop-off, so be careful.

Helman Deetjen built his Big Sur Inn at Castro Canyon from boards that washed up on the beach over thirty years ago. This is definitely not a Hilton hotel, but it has a rustic charm all its own. Deetjen's is open all year and has varied accommodations. The restaurant serves breakfast and lunch and candlelight dinners by reservation.

Post Hill, the site of the first coast Post Office and first school, was another bustling way station on the road from Monterey. Post's Campground is open during the summer and has campsites and trailer spaces near a stream.

"Nepenthe" is defined as "a potion used in ancient times to drown pain and sorrow." The steep path from the parking lot is worth the climb to view the seascape from the modern-day Nepenthe, 808 feet above sea level. Each summer thousands of tourists stop here to enjoy lunch or dinner, classical record concerts, fashion shows by local designers and evening folk dancing outdoors. This means it is usually crowded, though expensive; a

18

cup of coffee costs fifty cents. This was the original site of an old log house built by the Trails Club. Orson Welles purchased it as a castle for his movie queen, Rita Hayworth, but she preferred the Aga Khan and never lived here. Bill Fassett bought the property in 1947 and remodeled and expanded it for use as a restaurant. Nepenthe is open April through October only, but the Phoenix is open year-round and serves light food during winter months. Their gift shop has unusual local handcrafts and quality gifts of all kinds.

Up the steep curving hill is a gate leading to "Coastlands," a private residential area.

The Pfeiffer family had planned to find some good farmland farther south, but the winter of 1874 was so severe they were forced to remain in Sycamore Canyon. By spring they were settled in and decided to stay. Parts of "The Sandpiper," starring Elizabeth Taylor and Richard Burton, were filmed at Pfeiffer Beach. A path leads down to this white sandy beach and lagoon with its sea-carved caves. Take your coat; it's usually very windy here.

John Pfeiffer was the first permanent white settler at Big Sur. His homestead cabin is in Pfeiffer Big Sur State Park, 2,944 acres with eighty miles of hiking trails through a sylvan setting watered by the Big Sur River. This river is shown on early Spanish maps as Rio Grande del Sur (Big River of the South). Pfeiffer Park is also the hub for 500 miles of trails through the Los Padres National Forest, which encompasses 98,000 acres of wilderness. The Ventana Wilderness lies in the heartlands of the Santa Lucia Mountains. This is one of few places where the Santa Lucia fir (bristlecone fir) grows naturally and is also the southernmost end of the natural range of coast redwood. The Carmel, Arroyo Seco, Little and Big Sur Rivers run through Ventana. There is a 645-mile patchwork of fishing streams with native trout and some with rainbow trout stocked by the State Department of Parks and Recreation. Two sanctuaries have been established for the Cali-

*Carmelite Monastery stands serenely
above Carmel River Beach.*

fornia condor, an endangered species. Deer, wild boar and occasional black bear inhabit the forest, as well as numerous smaller animals. Grizzly bears were plentiful in Monterey County at one time. In fact, they were captured and pitted against bulls in a ring in Monterey. Now the State Department of Fish and Game estimates there are between twelve and fifteen bears in the county, most in Los Padres Forest.

Pfeiffer Big Sur State Park is a popular spot for outdoor enjoyment, a favorite of campers and always crowded in the summer months and on good weekends throughout the year. Hundreds of campers are turned away, so come early. Reservations for campsites can be made through Ticketron or by contacting any California State Park office. There are 218 developed campsites, trailer facilities, group campsites, picnic areas, swimming and fishing in the river and riding and hiking trails. It is an easy walk to Pfeiffer Falls in a fern-lined canyon. Below Pfeiffer Cabin is the rock-rimmed gravesite of the last Indian family to live at Big Sur. Mt. Manuel was named after Immanuel ("Manuel") Innocenti, who was a vaquero for Juan Bautista Cooper, owner of Rancho El Sur. On a clear day Mt. Manuel is the goal of many hikers. The trail climbs 4½ miles to an elevation of 3,100 feet for a splendid view of the coastline on one side and the vast wilderness on the other. Be sure to stay on marked trails; the park is full of poison oak.

Big Sur Lodge is a State concession with hotel-type accommodations and housekeeping cottages, a dining room, gift shop and general store. Fire permits, camping information, etc., are available at the Ranger Station. If you intend to hike into the Ventana Wilderness, be sure to sign in at this station.

The summer of 1972 was exceptionally dry. An illegal campfire started at Andrew Molera State Park grew to huge proportions, burning nearly 4,000 acres of the Los Padres National Forest. The Pfeiffer Park area miraculously escaped; only 200 acres of its forest land were burned. Most of the damage was concentrated on the Molera Ranch. At the height of the flames more than 1,700 firefighters, including many volunteers, were clearing firebreaks on both sides of the highway. Following the fire the State Department of Parks and Recreation supervised the placing of 13,500 sandbags to stem the anticipated flooding from fall rains. Sometimes Mother Nature's answer to not enough water is too much water. The rains came! In spite of the sandbags, this area was deluged with mudslides in October. An estimated 35,000 cubic yards of mud slid down from the burnt watershed; 10,000 cubic yards settled in Pfeiffer Park. This avalanche of mud was attributed to loose dirt and rocks left on the steep slopes which had been denuded by the forest fire in August. At one time a huge wall of mud six feet high and forty feet wide blocked the highway and covered the entire area, sweeping away cars and buildings. The garage and grocery store were demolished. The Big Sur Post Office was completely flattened; by December operation was resumed from a new mobile unit.

Reseeding on the hillsides with rye grass began immediately. High school students and other volunteers from all over the Peninsula pitched in to help Big Sur residents clean the mud out of their homes and businesses. A similar disaster occurred at Big Sur about twenty years ago, and the community bounced back, and it will do so again.

The residents of Big Sur are a medley of descendants of early settlers, businessmen catering to the tourist trade, Park and Forest Service employees, ranchers and farmers, artists, authors and artisans, and a changing population of hippies. Big Sur has no mayor and no town hall. Vounteers answer letters addressed to the non-existent chamber of commerce. Community matters are settled at civic meetings held at the Big Sur Grange Hall, which is also their gathering place for social events, movies, and square dances. Years ago the "Potluck Revue" was a simple neighborly production held to raise money to pay for the Grange Hall. While it is still called the "Potluck Revue," no dinner is served. Now this theatrical production with costumes rivalling the Broadway stage is presented on four nights. People come from miles around and tickets are precious.

Catholic masses are usually held Saturday afternoons and Sunday mornings at St. Francis of the Redwoods. This unusual church has a movable glass wall, making it possible to sit indoors or out where speakers are hidden in the towering trees. Big Sur Village also has an Episcopal Chapel.

Many kinds of accommodations are available in the Village area, and most are open year-round.

The 2,100 acres of Andrew Molera State Park, between Highway 1 and the ocean, extend on both sides of the Big Sur River to a point about two miles inland. This land was acquired in 1965, a gift to the State from Miss Frances Molera in memory of her brother. Until development funds are available, most of the land has been leased for use as a cattle ranch. Campfires are not permitted. Surfing and surf-fishing at the mouth of the river and freshwater fishing upstream are allowed.

The old County Road goes north out of Andrew Molera State Park over the mountain tops, coming out at the north end of Bixby Creek Bridge on Highway 1. It is a two-lane, hard-packed road, any car can make it, and it is a worthwhile scenic drive.

Before Point Sur Light Station started warning ships in 1889, many were smashed against the craggy rocks along the coast. A causeway links the Station with the mainland. During the rainy season this causeway is flooded, and the mighty rock looks like an island. Point Sur Light Station has a powerful first-order light, 50 feet above ground and 270 feet above sea level, which can be seen for 25 miles. The light has an intensity of 500,000 candles. The foghorn blasts every 60 seconds, and the Station is also equipped with a radio beacon. Coast Guard personnel are no longer re-

Big Sur's big surf.

quired to man this Station; the operation is entirely automatic. Visitors are not allowed.

Pico Blanco (elev. 3,710 ft.) dominates the skyline along the highway past the Little Sur River. There is a lovely lagoon where the river joins the sea, but this is all private property.

Hang onto your hat! Hurricane Point is the windiest spot on the whole highway. Be extremely careful, especially if you are driving a light car or a top-heavy camper or towing a trailer.

Bixby Creek Bridge is the most-photographed bridge along Highway 1. It is supposed to be the longest concrete arch span in the world, 718 feet long and 260 feet above Bixby Creek in the steep-walled canyon below. There are safe observation alcoves on the bridge which offer a breathtaking view of the Pacific. This is a fine vantage point for whale-watching. The sealanes are fifteen miles out; with binoculars you may be able to see a freighter or two. The ruins at Castle Rock at the northern edge of the canyon are the site of old Bixby Landing. During the late 1800's aerial cables brought lime, tanbark and redwood down to be loaded on steamers. The trail down to the creek mouth ends on a sandy beach. In September 1966 Mrs. Lyndon B. Johnson dedicated Highway 1 as California's first Scenic Highway. A plaque was placed at the south end of Bixby Bridge and promptly disappeared quite mysteriously. The plaque was inscribed with Robinson Jeffers' words:

"I, gazing at the boundaries of granite and spray,
The established sea marks, felt behind me,
Mountain and plain, the immense breadth of the continent,
Before me the mass and doubled stretch of water."

Palo Colorado means "redwood" in Spanish. There is a paved road leading into this narrow canyon lined with redwood and lush ferns with cabins along the creek. It goes to Bottchers Gap, the beginning of many hiking trails into the Ventana Wilderness, and beyond to Pico Blanco Boy Scout Camp. Sign in at the Ranger Station if you are hiking into Los Padres Forest. At the fenced-in helicopter landing, there is a striking view of Little Sur Valley, Double Cones, Pico Blanco and the Santa Lucia Range. You can also walk to the nearby lumber camp. Notley's Landing, across the highway from the entrance to Palo Colorado Canyon, was an early-day lumber boomtown and busy seaport.

Just north of the turn-off to Palo Colorado is the road leading to Rocky Point Restaurant and Cocktail Lounge. Their steaks and sea foods are excellent; reservations are recommended. The view from Rocky Point is nearly the same as from Vista Point to the north. Sea otters can be seen from both places.

Garrapata ("wood tick") Creek wanders through Garrapata Canyon to the ocean. This is a residential area with many rustic homes along the lushly bordered stream.

The path at Granite Canyon Bridge goes down to the sea where there is a small waterfall with natural arches nearby.

Little Malpaso Creek doesn't seem too forbidding now, but early accounts tell of the difficulties pioneers had crossing it.

High on the rocky cliffs overlooking the ocean is Highlands Inn, a honeymooners' haven for generations. They have a picturesque wedding chapel among the pines and honeymoon cottages. Stop for a drink if you can't afford their menu. Sunday brunch is a delightful experience, and the price is well worth it when you see the picture-postcard view from their dining room.

Spindrift Road winds toward the ocean past an exclusive residential area, including Kim Novak's home. Carmel Highlands is a long-established district of elegant homes, some on the rocky ledges and some hanging over the crashing surf. Yankee Point has a superb view of the craggy coastline and is especially good for whale-watching.

Francis McComas described Point Lobos as "the greatest meeting of land and water in the world," and you will agree. (You can see some of McComas' paintings at Del Monte Lodge at Pebble Beach and at the Roos/Atkins Store, Del Monte Center, Monterey.) It is said, too, that Robert Louis Stevenson used Point Lobos as a model for Spyglass Hill in "Treasure Island."

Magnificent Point Lobos State Reserve is a "must" on your itinerary. Wear warm comfortable clothing, low-heeled shoes and plan to spend several hours enjoying concentrated natural beauty. A map will be provided at the gate when you pay the entrance fee, 75¢ per car. Hikers are admitted free. Very few roads mar this primitive area. Most of it can be seen only on foot over unobtrusive trails. If you wish to smoke, do so in your car. Fires or smoking are not permitted in the park. Park your car only in a designated area, and remain on the marked trails. You may picnic, but there is no overnight camping. Swimming is permitted at China Cove, and boats can be launched at Whaler's Cove. Enjoy all of Point Lobos for its beauty is unequalled. Words are inadequate; Point Lobos must be experienced.

Point Lobos has had many owners. During the Mexican regime, this natural wonderland changed hands in a card game. In 1933, with the help of the Save-the-Redwoods League, it passed into the trusteeship of the State of California from an owner who appreciated the natural qualities of this well-preserved, almost primeval area. In 1968 the National Park Service designated this 1,250-acre Reserve a "Registered National Landmark." Point Lobos derives its name from its colonies of California and Steller's sea lions. You can hear their hoarse barking emanating from Punta de los Lobos Marinos (Point of the Seawolves). The California sea lion is the most intelligent of all sea lions and the one usually used in trained seal acts. The Steller is the largest and least controllable.

There are over 300 species of plants and 250 species of vertebrate and invertebrate animals and birds in this outdoor museum.

The Monterey Cypress, known in the Pliocene era, is making its last stand in the Monterey region. Only a half-mile strip is left in the world. There are two small areas where this famous tree still grows, one at Pebble Beach and the other here at Point Lobos. In the spring acres of wildflowers brighten the landscape. Sea otters are always playing offshore. Bird Island is a sanctuary for thousands of land and sea birds. Point Lobos is also the northernmost breeding ground of the California brown pelican. The conglomerate pebbles at Point Lobos, ranging in size from your thumbnail to several inches, are the only record known of rocks from the Eocene period.

State Rangers conduct guided tours twice daily in the summer and on a lesser schedule off season. Visitors are taken to six areas: the cypress grove, the pine wood, Bird Island, the North Shore Trail, Whaler's Cove or the sea lion area. In the summertime when weather and tides permit, there is also an early morning tidepool walk.

In the 1860's a whaling station was located at Whaler's Cove. This was a foul-smelling business with huge hunks of whale meat on the dock, cauldrons of boiling oil emitting dense black smoke, shouting men and screaming gulls. Whale-watching is preferable.

Point Lobos has the first undersea reserve in the nation, 750 acres of submerged land. With permission, underwater studies are carried on by individuals, universities, and private research groups. Skindivers must obtain permits (for looking only) at the park entrance.

You can see Point Lobos again in the movie "Jonathan Livingston Seagull." Much of it was filmed here with 13 Hollywood-trained, look-alike seagulls taking the part of one Jonathan, 55 "supporting" birds and 150 "extra" birds.

Japanese fishermen once harvested abalone in the semi-circular cove under San Jose Creek Bridge. On one of his expeditions Portola erected a cross here and buried a letter beneath it lamenting his failure to find Monterey Bay on that particular expedition.

The highway drops to sea level at Carmel River State Beach (106 acres), which is crowded during good weather with swimmers, surfers, skindivers, sunbathers, and surf-fishermen. The lagoon at the river mouth is better for small children. There are no facilities at the beach or the lagoon. When the river is running it is possible to paddle your canoe and kayak into the marshes for birdwatching.

The Carmelite Monastery is on the hill across from Carmel River State Beach. These nuns lead a strict, cloistered life. The nuns you see enjoying the beach are the Sisters of Notre Dame. The smaller building near the Monastery is Villa Angelica, their summer home.

The "Little Red Schoolhouse" is in an enviable setting of trees, sand dunes and beaches. This is Bay School, the cooperative nursery under the auspices of the Carmel Unified School District.

For 48 years the Odello family grew artichokes along both sides of the road on the flat plain near the Carmel River. Taxes on the land became exorbitant, and fungus and worms attacked the artichokes rendering much of the crop useless. The toxic spray used to control these blights might be harmful to people. As a consequence, the Odellos decided to sell their land to a developer. The developer's proposal to replace the artichoke fields with homes, a hotel and motel alarmed Peninsula citizens. A campaign is under way to raise funds to keep the open space and purchase the 150 acres closest to the ocean.

You have traveled through the incomparable Big Sur area, and you will do so again. Big Sur always beckons, but there is much more in store on the beautiful Monterey Peninsula, so upward to the Carmel hill and onward to Monterey.

*Stately Colton Hall, birthplace of
California's statehood.*

2 MONTEREY, THE OLD AND THE NEW

From the beginning, when it was first sighted in 1542 by Juan Rodrigues Cabrillo, a Portuguese navigator in the service of Spain, to the present day, Monterey's existence and fortunes have been tied to the bay that shares its name. Cabrillo noted this bay in his log but did not land on its tree-lined shores. The first visitor was the Spanish explorer, Sebastian Vizcaino, who named the area "Monterey" in honor of his sponsor, the Count of Monte Rey, and took possession of it in the name of Philip III of Spain. Vizcaino strongly recommended that the area be colonized as an outpost of the Spanish empire, but Philip ignored him. It wasn't until nearly two centuries later, on a June morning in 1770, that Captain Gaspar de Portola, Governor of Baja California, came by land with his small band of Spaniards, and Father Junipero Serra, a Franciscan monk, arrived by sea. They met on the beach and claimed the area once again for Spain. Father Serra set up the second Alta California Catholic Mission, while Captain Portola established the first California Presidio. Thus, the settlement of Monterey began with the cross and the sword as its symbols.

A cross was raised under a huge oak tree at the site of the original Mission, now San Carlos Cathedral on Church Street. The Mission was later re-established at its present location in Carmel because Father Serra wanted to remove his Indian neophytes to a quieter, more spiritual setting away from the rowdy Spanish soldiers in Monterey. Supplies were more readily available, and there were more artisans there to help train the Indians. The original Mission became known as the "Royal Presidio Chapel" and served the soldiers attached to the Presidio. San Carlos Cathedral, though small, is a typical example of Spanish-

31

Colonial architecture embellished with splendid Mexican folk art.

The first Presidio was built by Costanoan Indian laborers behind the present U.S.O. building on El Estero. In recent years members of the Monterey County Archaeological Society have uncovered its adobe foundations, and diggings have brought up many military and Indian artifacts. The area is fenced; you may look, but don't dig! Now the Presidio of Monterey, one of the oldest Army posts in the country, is situated on 409 acres of rolling hills which command a dramatic view of Monterey Bay. Once reverberating with the sound of bugles, marching feet and horses' hooves, today the Defense Language Institute, West Coast Branch, is the largest language school in the free world. Training is provided in 25 languages, including many dialects in each. The average daily enrollment is 2,500 students, representing all branches of the service. The 400-plus instructors are, with few exceptions, natives of the countries whose languages they teach. The small U.S. Army Museum on the hilltop features military memorabilia and is open to the public from 11:00 a.m. to 1:00 p.m., and 2:00 to 5:00 p.m. Wednesday, Thursday and Friday; from 10:00 a.m. to 5:00 p.m. on Saturdays and Sundays; closed Mondays and Tuesdays. Be sure to observe the strictly enforced traffic rules—this is a military reservation.

The ten-foot granite cross at the entrance to the Presidio marks one of the most historic spots on the Monterey Peninsula. It was erected in 1906 to mark the approximate site where Vizcaino and his men celebrated Mass upon their arrival in 1602. At this same place Portola and Father Serra held services when they met in Monterey to found a new Spanish colony.

With game plentiful, the forest thick with timber, the land fertile, water abundant and temperatures moderate, the colony could not help but prosper. At first Monterey was only a fort. Five years after the establishment of the Presidio, soldiers' families settled and Monterey became a pueblo. When Mexico obtained independence from Spain in 1821, Monterey served under a second flag as the capital of Mexican California and eventually the capital of Alta California and remained so until 1854 when Sacramento became the permanent seat.

You can sense Monterey's fascinating past along the "Path of History." Following the orange-red line painted on the streets will take you to 45 historic sites in this cradle of California history. Some are private offices and residences, but many are open to the public. A few have gift or antique shops and restaurants. Maps for this self-guided driving or strolling tour are available at the Monterey History and Art Association offices at Custom House Plaza or from the Monterey Peninsula Chamber of Commerce, 2030 Fremont (Fairgrounds Travelodge). This Chamber and their Visitors and Convention Bureau serves the entire Monterey Peninsula and has a wealth of free brochures and maps which will make your visit even more pleasurable.

In June 1846, during the war with Mexico, Commodore John Drake Sloat had the American flag raised over the Custom House, claiming all of Alta California for the United States. This famous adobe, built by the Mexican Government in 1814, has exhibits from the three periods of California's history when Monterey was the capital. Four flags fly over the Plaza: Spanish, Mexican, American, and California's Bear Flag. Many special events are held here, including the Re-enactment of Sloat's Landing each July.

California's first Constitutional Convention was held at Colton Hall on Pacific Street in 1849. At that time it was the most pretentious building in the whole state; in fact, it still is a distinguished building. Colton Hall is open to the public daily from 10:00 a.m. to 5:00 p.m. and has an excellent historical museum on the second floor. It also houses Monterey's city offices.

With the start of the Gold Rush, Monterey's fortunes ebbed as San Francisco, closer to the mines, became California's principal port and political and commercial center. By the mid-1800's, however, Monterey regained some of its prestige as an important whaling port. The Old Whaling Station on Decatur Street was built as a private residence in 1855. Later it became a boarding house for a group of Portuguese whalers. They formed the Monterey Whaling Company and devised improved methods for harpooning the humpback and California gray whales. Vessels totaling 640 moved between the California coast and the Hawaiian Islands. Some of the harpooners were natives from the South Seas with painted bodies and colorful dress. Fences made of whalebones were common. The sidewalk in front of the Old Whaling Station is made from them, and the mantle over the door to California's First Theatre is a large whalebone. The price of whale oil declined and whalebone use was limited; by 1877 the entire Pacific Coast whaling fleet was reduced to forty ships. Since 1937 gray whales have been completely protected by international agreement. They still ply their passage along the coast on annual trips to Mexican waters in November, returning north along the same route in March.

In the middle of the 19th century sea otters were hunted off the Central Coast for their desirable fur. This was an important economic factor to Monterey. The otter population in the Pacific once numbered two million, but by 1867 they had been hunted to near extinction. Fortunately, the otter, too, has reappeared and has increased in numbers under Government protection. Like the migrating whales, they put on sea shows for delighted audiences. Rafts of otters can be seen off Cannery Row, along the Pacific Grove and Pebble Beach shorelines and at Point Lobos. The most remarkable feature about the sea otter is that it is the only marine animal known to use a tool. Floating on his back, the otter places a large flat rock on his stomach, holds a shellfish, such as a mussel or turban snail, with both of his paws and then brings it down hard on the rock to crack it. Surely there is no more cunning sight in local waters than that of a mother sea otter floating leisurely on her back in a kelp bed and cuddling her baby, like a wet teddy bear, on her chest while both are rocked by gentle offshore waves.

With the whales and otters gone, Monterey again looked to its bay for resource. The city became world-famous as the sardine capital of the western hemisphere, adding a new mystique to Monterey's reputation and a colony of Sicilian fishermen to its population. In a peak year over 200,000 tons of sardines (pilchard) were processed in the plants on Cannery Row. The silver fish filled the city's coffers with gold until the mid-forties when they mysteriously disappeared from the bay. There are many theories about this phenomenon, some based on fact perhaps, others pure fancy. No one really knows why they left. A small fishing fleet still chugs out of the harbor in the early mornings and brings back catches of cod, yellowfin, squid, salmon, shrimp or crab, in season, to be sold on Fisherman's Wharf and to restaurants throughout the Peninsula.

Monterey's geographical location makes it the hub of the Peninsula. Today it is a city of 27,000 deliberately uncommercial, shunning any form of air-polluting industry. Its revenue is derived from the Peninsula's military installations, from its institutions of higher learning, from a series of annual events and its scenic, artistic and historic atmosphere which make it attractive to travelers.

There is a distinctive building design in the architectural world called "the Monterey style," a reminder of Spanish and Mexican times, plus a little Johnny-come-lately influence. The term "adobe" refers to a house built of mud mixed with straw, which retained heat in winter and kept the sun's rays from penetrating in the summer. Whitewash (lime) was applied to the outside walls to form a sort of plaster. Land was cheap, so a typical house was built with plenty of space around it, usually in the center of

Monterey's fishing fleet at dawn.

a courtyard, and constructed crosswise to the compass letting the sun shine for some part of each day into every room. It had two stories with living quarters downstairs and bedrooms upstairs. A balcony extended halfway or all the way around the upper story. In the Spanish-Mexican period, the stairs to the bedrooms were usually outside. Although it is said this encouraged elopements, such a design had its practical aspects. The returning master could clean up without tracking dirt through the ground floor rooms. He could also sneak in and out unsuspected if circumstances necessitated. New England influence later placed the stairs on the inside.

Some early Yankee settlers were ships' carpenters who built their houses of pine and redwood so plentiful in the area. Dirt and tiled floors were replaced with wood, and shutters were put on the outside rather than inside. They continued the custom of building their doors in pairs with each single door too small for a person to pass through. There was wisdom in this as a good protective device. Eventually the practical New Englanders replaced Monterey's bougainvillea-draped adobe·walls with plain white picket fences.

Excellent examples of the original Monterey-type homes, many now converted into office buildings, can be seen along the Path of History. They are a credit to the members of the Monterey History and Art Association who saved most of the original homes from destruction and authentically restored them. Each spring the Association holds an Adobe House Tour with hostesses dressed in Spanish-Colonial costumes serving as guides.

Pacific House at the intersection of Calle Principal and Alvarado is a long, two-story adobe with a characteristic balcony on four sides. Originally it was a hotel and saloon for seafaring men. The house and grounds cover one-third of a city block. There was a bull and bear pit arena here during Spanish-Mexican times; now it is Memory Garden where Monterey celebrates its birthday with a "Merienda" each June. The lower floor is a public museum of Monterey lore.

If you are driving into Monterey from the north on Highway 1, be sure to stay in the right lane as there is a tricky spot on the freeway where the left lane suddenly branches off without previous warning and goes to Carmel.

Points of interest turn up immediately as you enter the city on Fremont Street. On the right is the Naval Postgraduate School. Here over 1,500 officers of the U.S. Navy, Marine Corps, Army, Air Force, and Coast Guard, as well as officers from 22 allied countries, are educated for leadership in the modern world of technology, science and management. The picturesque old buildings and tailored grounds, with a swan lake and families of peacocks roaming at will, are of particular interest. This was once the most deluxe resort on the West Coast and even now is often referred to as "the old Del Monte Hotel." It was opened in 1880 by the redoubtable four San Francisco multi-millionaires: Leland Stanford, Mark Hopkins, Collis P. Huntington and Charles Crocker. The elite of San Francisco and Southern California arrived in their private cars at the hotel's railroad station. The station now stands deserted while the hotel buildings have been converted into administration offices, classrooms for students and living quarters for faculty members. All enjoy the elegant Roman plunge, the tennis courts, and the well-tended acres of gardens where, in the early 1900's, millionaires and their ladies mingled with a new type of society. The Del Monte Hotel never quite lifted Monterey to the social eminence enjoyed by Newport and Saratoga on the Eastern seaboard. When World War II created a scarcity of help and patrons, it was leased to the U.S. Navy in 1940 as a pre-flight training center. It was closed definitely as a hostelry in 1951 when the Government bought the hotel and surrounding acreage as the location of the newly expanded Naval Postgraduate School.

38

There are fifteen fine hotels on the Monterey Peninsula. You may find that it doesn't cost any more to stay in a hotel and enjoy all of its luxurious amenities than it does to stay in a better motel. Six of these hotels are in Monterey. The Holiday Inn in its sand-dune setting, just off the freeway on the way into town, is like no other Holiday Inn. It is at the water's edge with an all-encompassing view of Monterey Bay. Del Monte Hyatt House (420 rooms) is the largest hotel on the Peninsula and headquarters for many conventions. Their fifteen oak-studded acres border Del Monte Golf Course (public), the oldest course west of the Mississippi. Casa Munras Garden Hotel is a cluster of attractive adobe buildings in a garden setting in downtown Monterey.

Monterey Peninsula College is on the tree-clad hillside overlooking Fremont Street. This is a two-year junior college with an average enrollment of 2,200 day students and 2,400 evening students and one of the State's finest.

To the right is Lake El Estero where fat, spoiled coots and ducks make their home. Children love feeding them bread crusts and leftover picnic goodies. Ducks can nip fingers, so be wary. Pedal boats and canoes can be rented on the far side of the lake. If you are under sixteen, you may fish from the bridge. On the shore across the bridge is a shady picnic area with tables, benches and grills.

Dennis the Menace Playground, designed by Hank Ketcham, Dennis' creator, and built by the Monterey Peninsula Junior Chamber of Commerce, is at Lake El Estero and a certain stop if you have children along. Its landmark is a real stationary Southern Pacific locomotive for scrambling over and pretend-engineering. There are two wading pools, unusual swings, slides and tunnels and imaginative mazes, all free to enjoy.

After you have viewed San Carlos Cathedral on Church Street, turn right on Abrego. Look for the antique jeweler's clock and the high blue gates which open to the Clock Restaurant, a former

*John Steinbeck made Monterey's
Cannery Row famous.*

adobe carriage house and one of the better restaurants on the Peninsula. Patrons may dine inside the restaurant with its lively decor and cozy bar or outside in the flower-bowered courtyard.

At the corner of Tyler and Munras is pleasant Jules Simoneau Plaza with fountains, flowers and benches. Simoneau owned the house where Robert Louis Stevenson lived and befriended the destitute young writer by providing him with free meals at his restaurant which stood on this spot.

Stevenson House on Houston Street is interesting for several reasons. Robert Louis Stevenson lived here in the autumn of 1879 while courting his future wife, Fanny Osborne, ten years his senior and the divorced mother of two children. She was visiting her sister and escaping from her unhappy first marriage. Now a State Historical Monument, the Stevenson House is an outstanding example of an adobe dwelling. Its rooms are filled with accurate furnishings and bric-a-brac of the 19th century and Stevenson memorabilia. Your youngsters will be fascinated by the children's room because it contains their small-sized period clothing and antique toys. Stevenson House is significant, too, because it has a ghost or two. One figure is said to be Jules Simoneau's wife who is sometimes seen standing at the top of the stairway. At other times the shadowy romantic figure of Robert Louis Stevenson himself has appeared in the room he once occupied.

On Hartnell Street "halfway between the jail and the hospital" is Gallatin's, an historic adobe and the Peninsula's only Holiday Magazine award winner year after year for distinctive dining. Expect to enjoy exciting and expensive continental cuisine. The bar opens at 4:00 p.m. and closes when the piano player goes home, and dinner is served from 5:00 p.m. to midnight. You'll need reservations, of course.

Alvarado is considered Monterey's main street (one-way). If shopping is your goal, after you have checked out the stores on

41

Alvarado Street, go to the expansive Del Monte Shopping Center (off Highway 1 traveling south) where you will find everything from a discount drug store to a good-sized Macy's, even a branch of Saks Fifth Avenue, but no dime store. In downtown Monterey you may get the feeling that there are lots of parking places but no reason to park. Be assured there are many reasons. Blocks of old buildings have been leveled to make room for a huge convention center, hotel and attendant businesses to be built in the future. You may also get the feeling that it is nigh impossible to get to where you want to go from where you are. Be of stout heart—it's possible!

Calle Principal runs parallel to Alvarado. The Allen Knight Maritime Museum at 500 Calle Principal reflects Monterey's nautical past. This museum was named after a former Mayor of Carmel who collected its maritime exhibits, ship models and sea lore during his lifetime. Admission is free. Hours are 1:00 to 4:00 p.m. weekdays and 2:00 to 4:00 p.m. Saturdays and Sundays, closed Mondays and holidays.

If you follow Jefferson Street straight to the top of the hill to the grassy fields, you will find city-owned and operated Veterans Memorial Park with complete facilities for overnight camping and daytime picnicking. There is access to this park, too, from Highway 68 which runs through the forest between Highway 1 and Pacific Grove.

Alvarado Street extends to the Custom House Plaza in the heart of the waterfront sector with plentiful parking in the area. You can wander through expanses of red-roofed white adobes surrounded by seasonal flowers. Plane trees provide shade and a Spanish fountain a lyrical note. The gazebo in the center doubles as a stage. Adjacent to the Plaza is a boccie ball court where retired Sicilian fishermen play their national game which resembles outdoor bowling.

A few blocks up the hill from the Custom House Plaza at the corner of Scott and Pacific is California's First Theatre. In the middle of the 19th century it was a saloon and sailors' boarding house operated by Jack Swan. In 1847 a small group of Army volunteers presented two minstrel shows, and Swan's bar became the first building on the Pacific Coast in which paid dramatic performances were staged. The Gold Coast Troupers present live old-time melodramas here Wednesday through Sunday evenings in the summer and on Fridays and Saturdays during the winter. Their box office is open summer afternoons so you can reserve tickets. Sip sarsaparilla, hiss the villain and cheer the hero. It's wholesome fun for everyone.

The entrance to Fisherman's Wharf is near the Custom House. The attractions on the wharf are geared to family fun. Sandwiched between fish markets, boat sales, rentals and excursion concessions and restaurants are gift shops and bazaars, art galleries, a book store and candy shop. There is also a small sea-life museum, and plans are under way for a live production theater. The many-colored buildings perched on old pilings have a certain charm. Graceful gulls circle overhead and pampered sea lions bark and beg from the waters below.

Most of the restaurants on the wharf serve sand dabs, a local fish delicacy. Lunch is sometimes a better bargain than their candlelit dinners. There are a few happy exceptions like the Abalonetti, a little Mediterranean cafe which serves only freshly caught fish and seasonal specialties, and one or two other restaurants which you may discover yourself.

Of course, you want to buy a souvenir to take home, but don't settle for an impractical ashtray with a decal on it and stamped "made in Japan" on the bottom. There are limitless shops all over the Monterey Peninsula, including here on Fisherman's Wharf, at Cannery Row and especially in Carmel, which sell inexpen-

*Roberta Flack and Quincy Jones electrify their
audience at the Monterey Jazz Festival.*

sive locally-made crafts typical of the area. Use your good taste and good judgment when choosing, however. Just because you bought the item in Monterey or Carmel doesn't necessarily mean it's a work of art.

The Jolly Rogue Restaurant with the San Martin Wine-Tasting Room downstairs will identify the entrance to Municipal Wharf No. 2. This pier was built in 1926 to accommodate larger ships coming into the harbor. This is the working wharf with whole-sale fish warehouses at its end, where you can watch commercial boats unloading their catches of tuna, sole, salmon, cod, kingfish, anchovies and herring. If you want to do some dropline fishing yourself for tom cod or sunfish, bait is free with rod rentals on both wharves, and no license is required for saltwater fishing from a public pier. Arrangements for deep-sea fishing trips can be made on both wharves. You can launch your own boat from Wharf No. 2

The Monterey Peninsula Yacht Club and its marina filled with bouncing small craft is at Wharf No. 2. Next to it, down the stairs and underneath the pier, is The Windjammer. This little nautical restaurant and bar has a roll-top deck. The food is good and the activity great. If you're staying at a hotel or motel, call The Windjammer and their "shoreboat" (a free courtesy bus) will pick you up and return you to your quarters.

Monterey Municipal Beach east of the wharf is a sandy mile-long stretch. A lifeguard is on duty in the area closest to the pier during summer months. The warm shallow water in this spot is good wading for small children. The whole beach is good for sunbathing and picnicking. No open fires are allowed, but you may use a camp stove or hibachi. Monterey's Fourth of July fireworks are set off here.

Follow the shoreline below Presidio hill to reach one of the most celebrated streets in the world—Cannery Row. Until Nobel-

and Pulitzer-prizewinning author, John Steinbeck, drew world-wide attention to it, it was known as Ocean View Avenue. Steinbeck's novel "Cannery Row," written in 1944, immortalized its oily setting and offbeat cast of characters which were actually a part of Monterey's booming sardine industry. Cannery Row has not changed so much that you cannot imagine "Doc" Ed Ricketts (a real life character) and his cronies reeling up the wooden stairs to his Pacific Biological Laboratory at 800 Cannery Row, now a private club. Presidio soldiers no longer come to the Bear Flag building for the same purpose; walls between the tiny upstairs rooms have been removed to form suites of offices. Lee Chong's grocery store is as fascinating as it was in the pilchard days; it's filled with collectibles from the sardine era and antiques from earlier times. You can still eat at La Ida's Cafe, now Kalisa's International Restaurant. Dora's name was really "Flora," and you can still get a frothy glass of beer and a bar lunch, not free, but cheap, at Flora's Bar. Above all, the current-day Cannery Row characters are equally as colorful as Steinbeck's fictional ones.

Oldtimers are the first to tell you that they had no personal regrets about the sardines' departure. In Monterey's heyday when the canneries worked round the clock, a malodor hung over the city for days at a time. Residents held cologned handkerchiefs to their noses when going out. Cannery Row was certainly no tourist mecca in those days. A hush fell over the Row as the canneries folded, and Monterey suffered another shock to its economy. Monterey recovered, the street was reincarnated with the new and the old standing side by side, and Cannery Row became one of the major attractions of the Monterey Peninsula.

The old Coast Guard pier at the start of Cannery Row is always crowded with skindivers. They get in and out of wet suits and inflate their bright-colored rafts next to their parked cars which jam the vacant bayshore lot during daylight hours. Otters and sea lions entertain here, too, to the amusement of the divers and a gallery of spectators.

Some dilapidated cannery buildings, with their salt-stained, cracked windows and weather-worn names on their sides, stand idle. This is the way the sardines left them. Other canneries have been renovated and now house an assortment of businesses. Go around a curve and suddenly you are in the midst of a new and different Cannery Row lined with restaurants and cocktail lounges, art galleries, specialty shops and antique stores.

Parking is a never-ending problem. While there are many public lots, on busy summer days and winter weekends, you may have to park several blocks up the hill.

You'll never go hungry or thirsty on Cannery Row. Some of the Peninsula's finest restaurants and cocktail lounges are here, and it is also the center for much of the area's night life. Some regulars perform on the Row, like belting Barbara Kelly, the warbler at The Warehouse, and versatile Jerry Winters and Sioux Scott at the Outrigger who entertain with their improvised comedy routines and Broadway show songs. The best way to see what's happening around the Peninsula is to check the entertainment pages of the Monterey Peninsula Herald or pick up a free copy of Key Magazine, available at many hotels, motels and restaurants.

The plush crimson decor, nostalgic "wall of fame" and the 110-year-old carved bar are a perfect background for the excellent cuisine at The Sardine Factory. Traditional entrees and original specialties on their luncheon and dinner menus have an Italian flair and are immensely popular and highly recommended.

For over twenty years Neil DeVaughn's has been the place to go for a thick, juicy steak or outstanding sea food specialties. Dinner reservations are in order here.

The continental lunch and dinner menus at York of Cannery

Row (in the Bear Flag building) have a subtle English influence. This is a beautifully appointed restaurant with a pleasantly-mellow atmosphere.

The luncheon Buffet-by-the-Bay at Mark Thomas' Outrigger is a bargain. Besides, you can enjoy a Mai-Tai beforehand and a constant show put on by otters, birds, boats, and skindivers. On a dreary day there is no cozier spot than the Outrigger's lanai. No matter the weather, the view is superb. This is the only restaurant on the Row jutting out over the water. When the surf is angry, waves crash under the dining room and spray the picture windows. Polynesian food and drinks are the Outrigger's sit-down dinner specialties, as well as American cuisine.

The Fish Market in Steinbeck Circle has a large window in the floor for wave-watching. They feature Italian family lunches and dinners, emphasizing sea foods.

Mexican decor contributes to Tia Maria's waterfront atmosphere. Costumed senoritas serve south-of-the-border dishes and strolling musicians create a romantic mood.

It's fun for the whole family at The Warehouse—pizza, spaghetti and ravioli—in a roaring-twenties setting complete with honky-tonk band and silent film flicks.

Cannery Row Square comprises two, three-storied buildings with an overhead walkway between. There are a number of restaurants here, Lisbon Pub, Golden Dragon, Chez Felix, and several interesting small cafes. Be sure to stop for a drink at the zany Boiler Room, topside. As its name implies, it is a replica of a ship's boiler room and the after-hours rock music is just as noisy.

Cannery Row Square, patterned after San Francisco's Ghirardelli Square, houses many galleries and specialty shops. The Whole Earth Craft Center, above The Warehouse, is open from noon to midnight, except Mondays, and is a complex of shops featuring, for the most part, locally-made handcrafts of all kinds.

There is probably no theater in your hometown like the 812

Cinema. Recline on huge pillows as you watch foreign, classic or underground films.

One lone cannery continues to operate at the end of Cannery Row, when once eighteen canneries worked night and day serviced by a fleet of a hundred fishing boats. More than 4,000 names were on the membership rolls of the Cannery Workers Union. Each plant had its particular whistle which blew at any time to summon its workers. If the sardines ever return, only one cannery will be ready to welcome them.

Three blocks up the hill from Cannery Row is the section called "New Monterey," a name left over from other days because it is actually one of the older parts of the city. Lighthouse Avenue is the main street and shopping district. Here you will find a half-dozen antique stores. The workshop of the Peninsula Potters is at Lighthouse and Hoffman. Scholze Park, to the east, has a children's playground. Across the street is Consuelo's, an excellent Mexican restaurant with exceptional service, in a beautifully restored Victorian mansion. To the west, a couple of blocks across the border into Pacific Grove, is the Mont-Grove Craft Guild with the largest selection of local crafts and imports under one roof on the Peninsula.

Many annual events, including the famed Monterey Jazz Festival, are held at the Monterey County Fairgrounds. Unlike most fairgrounds, this one offers an atmosphere of exceptional beauty and relaxation with its rolling lawns and huge oak trees. The exciting Laguna Seca Sports Car Races are held three times a year at the track alongside Highway 68.

Green Gables, one of Pacific Grove's restored Victorians.

3 PICTURESQUE PACIFIC GROVE

The Methodists had been seeking a suitable spot for a seaside Christian resort for some time, and they found it on this northern-most point of the Monterey Peninsula. Many years before Indian tribes from the inland vacationed in the groves of pines and oaks and restocked their larders with mussels, abalone and fish. In 1875 a group of ministers from the Methodist Episcopal Church in San Francisco formed the Pacific Grove Retreat Association and put an almost indelible mark on the customs and laws of the city. Land was purchased from Southern Pacific and from David Jacks, and a tent city was laid out on 30' x 60' lots. Furnished tents rented from $2.25 to $5.50 a week. At the close of each summer season the tents were carefully packed and stored at Chautauqua Hall, 17th and Central Avenue, now used by the Boy Scouts and for many community events.

The Retreat became a haven for other denominations, too. The Episcopalians, Catholics, Congregationalists, the Christian Church, and the Salvation Army all established churches here before the turn of the century. In the early 1900's the Christian Scientists, Baptists, and First Assembly of God built their churches.

Southern Pacific excursions from the San Francisco Bay area brought hundreds of people to Pacific Grove; the round trip cost one dollar. The Methodists fenced their little compound, rang the curfew bell at 9:00 p.m. and locked the gates. There were rigid rules concerning dancing, drinking and public bathing. Bathing suits had to be made of "opaque material, which shall be worn in such a manner as to preclude form. All such bathing suits shall be provided with double crotches or with skirts of ample size to cover the buttocks." Whatever laws weren't on the books were understood anyway. Robert Louis Stevenson wrote about Pacific Grove: "Thither, in the warm season, crowds came to enjoy a life of teetotalism, religion, and flirtation, which I am willing to think blameless and agreeable."

Expenses for running the campground were paid by selling lots. Small cottages sprang up everywhere and can be seen along the narrow streets between Lovers Point (sometimes called Point Aulon on maps) and Pine Avenue. Year-round residents built handsome Victorian mansions. Within ten years Pacific Grove became a cultural center. The first Chautauqua (an assembly for educational purposes, combining lectures, entertainment, etc.) was held in June 1879. The city hosted three Presidents, Benjamin Harrison, William McKinley, and Theodore Roosevelt.

In 1880 State Senator Benjamin Langford, tired of unlocking the gate, took an ax to it; thus Pacific Grove dramatically joined the rest of the Monterey Peninsula. Fifty years later Dr. Julia Platt, the city's first and only lady Mayor, took an ax to another gate at Lovers of Jesus Point. The city later purchased this beach property, and it is now known simply as "Lovers Point." A Christian campground blossomed into a charming city and became incorporated in 1889. Pacific Grove now has a population nearing 15,000.

Provincial Pacific Grove has relaxed at last. For 96 years the sale of alcohol was prohibited. In spite of the continuing efforts of the Pacific Grove Retreat Association to keep the town dry, in 1969 voters broke loose from this restriction and today liquor is sold in what was then California's last dry town.

There is a pleasing blend of old-fashioned and contemporary architecture with many beautiful homes typical of both eras. It is easy to find your way around. Drive through the residential sections above Ocean View Boulevard. If you get lost, just head toward the water and you will be back on your itinerary.

A number of movies with New England settings have been made in Pacific Grove. Several have been filmed at the LaPorte Mansion, 1030 Lighthouse Avenue, built in the 1880's by an Englishman who called it "Pinehurst Manor." Annually in April, there is a two-day Victorian House Tour. If you don't happen to be here in April, have dinner at Maison Bergerac (the Hart Mansion), 19th and Lighthouse Avenue, which was built in 1890. Not only is it a fine family-owned and operated French restaurant, but it is a beautifully restored Victorian home. The menu is posted out front. Only thirty persons can be accommodated in an evening, so reservations are necessary.

Pacific Grove is known as "Butterfly Town U.S.A." and rightly so. For over a hundred years tens of thousands of bright orange and black monarch butterflies (Anosia plexipus) have migrated each October from the northern Pacific states, British Columbia and southern Alaska to winter in the groves of trees, only to fly away in March. This annual miracle is one of nature's mysteries and not yet scientifically explained. The Pacific Grove Museum of Natural History, at Forest and Central, has an exhibit showing the monarchs' migration pattern. The butterflies hang in huge clusters like dried leaves in the tall pines in Butterfly Trees Park on Lighthouse Avenue, at the Alder Street side of Washington Park and in scattered trees throughout the city. On sunny days what you might think is a dead tree will suddenly come alive in a burst of color which slowly disseminates into lazy, velvet-winged butterflies fluttering over town gardens. Leave your butterfly net at home! There is a $500 fine or a jail sentence for molesting a monarch butterfly in Pacific Grove. Hundreds of costumed school children herald the return of the monarchs every October by marching in the much-photographed Butterfly Parade. Gordon Newell's granite sculpture of a monarch stands in Lovers Point Park, one of few monuments in the country honoring the insect world.

Monarchs of Pacific Grove.

David Avenue is the dividing line between Monterey and Pacific Grove. It is simple to drive to the end of Cannery Row, jog to the right and you will be on Ocean View Boulevard. So let's peruse picturesque Pacific Grove . . .

Within a block will be the boat works. Peek in if you like (they won't mind), and you'll see ferro cement boats a-building. Many of the fishing boats working out of Monterey Bay were built here in years past before cement was used for this purpose.

Hopkins Marine Station on China Point, operated by Stanford University, specializes in the study of intertidal life. It was the first marine laboratory on the Pacific Coast and the third in the nation. Scan Monterey Bay and you may see their ship which operates in all kinds of weather.

For more than fifty years a Chinese village thrived on China Point but burned to the ground quite mysteriously in 1903. Its settlers originally came to work in the Santa Lucia mines during the Gold Rush days and drifted to the coast to resume a more familiar occupation, fishing. After the fire the Chinese established a community on Alvarado Street in Monterey. The Feast of Lanterns, held in Pacific Grove the last weekend of July, is based on an Oriental legend. Villagers searched with lighted boats and lanterns for the Mandarin's lovesick daughter who was forbidden to marry her peasant sweetheart and ran off to drown herself. The Feast of Lanterns appropriately acknowledges the legend with a four-day city-wide celebration, including a lantern procession, a lighted boat parade and the crowning of Queen Topaz, culminating with a huge fireworks display.

On the corner of 5th Street is Green Gables, built in 1878, now authentically restored and operated as a guest house. Note that it faces three directions on three levels.

Let the kids out to run at Berwick Park, the large grassy area on the shore side between Hopkins Marine Station and Lovers Point, great for tossing frisbies or playing touch football.

Lovers Point Park just ahead has picnic facilities, a volley ball court, children's pool and access to the sheltered beach. This is one of the few safe wading and swimming beaches on the Monterey Peninsula. Be forewarned; the water's cold! In the summertime, for a small charge, the glass-bottom boats will take you out to view the underwater gardens offshore. In spite of the nippy average 55° temperature of the surface water, hardy skindivers enjoy this spot, and surfers skim the huge waves when they break off the point. Rock fishing is good on the far side of the pier.

Many national publications have featured Pacific Grove's "Magic Carpet of Mysembryanthemum." A solid mass of pink and lavender ice plant, interspersed with clumps of geraniums and marguerites, blooms from late April through August along the cliffs beyond Lovers Point. This sight can make your whole visit to Pacific Grove worthwhile.

The three-mile shoreline is spectacular any time of the year, equally as beautiful as Seventeen Mile Drive, and free. Pacific Grove is one of the few California cities which owns its own shoreline. Because of continuing beach erosion and the disappearance of many small marine animals in recent years, collecting of all kinds is prohibited on these beaches. Park at the turn-out points. Feed the squirrels and chipmunks, but watch your fingers or you may need a tetanus shot. Look for sea otters frolicking in the kelp beds. Climb down on the rocks to the water, but be extremely cautious. The surf is unsafe; the undertow is quick and treacherous. If you feel like walking, there is a safe path between the street and the beach, with welcome benches along the way, from Lovers Point to the Lighthouse Reservation.

The 18-hole Pacific Grove Golf Links, the only city-owned course on the Monterey Peninsula, is a fairly easy course and the least expensive of the public courses on the Peninsula. Little Crespi Pond at the edge of the course is a haven for a variety of land and sea birds and is notable because it is a fresh-water pond yet close to salt water. Also, there is a herd of deer roaming the golf greens.

If you have little ones along, you might turn left at Lighthouse Avenue, go a few blocks and drive through El Carmelo Cemetery. This isn't as morbid as it sounds. The entire Peninsula abounds with wildlife, and you may see deer nibbling at the flowers in front of the headstones in the cemetery, sort of "Santa's summer home."

A lard oil lamp first shone at Point Piños Light Station in 1855 and later a kerosene lamp. Now the 29,000 candlepower third-order electric light is visible for fifteen miles. It is 43 feet above ground and 89 feet above water. This is the oldest lighthouse in continuous operation on the West Coast and was a landmark for galleons taking the north circle route down the California Coast to Mexico. The tower was damaged extensively in the infamous 1906 earthquake and had to be rebuilt. The Station houses a small museum of Coast Guard history and is open to the public Saturdays and Sundays from 1:00 to 4:00 p.m. Directly below the lighthouse is the air diaphragm horn fog signal. Being on the road next to it when the foghorn blasts will give you a jolt, to say the least.

Beyond Point Piños, this site of many pre-radar shipwrecks, you will be on the ocean side of Pacific Grove. A herd of seals, an otter or two and sometimes a sea lion inhabit the cove at the foot of Arena Avenue.

Adjoining the city is Asilomar State Beach and Conference Grounds, sixty acres of sand dunes and pine trees, where hundreds of conventions are held annually. It was originally founded by the Y.W.C.A. over forty years ago, but now belongs to the State of California and is run by Asilomar Operating Corporation, a non-profit organization. It is the only place of its kind in the State Park system. In 1969 the California State Department of Parks and Recreation established a Training Center here for state

Pacific Grove's sweeping shoreline.

rangers and park employees. This is formal classroom training with courses lasting one to five weeks and an average enrollment of twenty students. A new training facility, which will expand their services, is being built by Asilomar Operating Corp. and is scheduled to open in September 1973. It will also house a research library for scholars.

Asilomar State Beach, between Point Piños and Del Monte Forest, is invigorating. Hope you brought your old shoes! Poke around in the tidepools, run on the beach, play in the sand, watch the surfers if the surf's up, do some surf-fishing, eat your sandy sandwiches and just generally enjoy a real ocean beach. This is where Doc gathered his specimens from the "Great Tidepool" mentioned in "Cannery Row." Here, too, the surf is unsafe for swimming. There are over 210 species of algae on Asilomar Beach, more varieties than any beach on the coast, because the northern and southern waters merge here. Please remember that California State law makes it illegal to collect any tidal invertebrates in state parks, recreation areas, state beaches and reserves. No general collecting is allowed between the mean high tide mark and 1,000 feet beyond mean low tide without a special permit, granted only to qualified researchers. Flowers, rocks, plants, animals and other natural features are protected by law. Driftwood may be collected in state parks because it is not considered part of the natural environment.

You will be traveling east on Sunset Drive, State Highway 68. If you like jelly beans, free bicycling, water beds with velvet blankets and an ocean view, you'll like the Beachcomber Inn. They also have wheelchair rooms. Kalisa's International Restaurant is here with a menu similar to Kalisa's on Cannery Row. For a Korean dinner, try the Sunset Restaurant at Sunset Center. If you are staying in Pacific Grove, visit Fitzgerald's Gallery, 2102 Sunset Drive, but save most of your gallery browsing for Carmel.

Point Pinos Light Station, the oldest operating lighthouse on the West Coast.

The First United Methodist Church was built in 1963 on five wooded acres. The original Methodist Church, which doubled as a town hall in the Retreat days, was in the downtown area and was torn down in the early sixties. The new church has an inspiring stained-glass "Resurrection Window," emphasizing parts of monarch butterfly wings. You are welcome to visit the sanctuary of Pacific Grove's founding church.

If you follow Highway 68 (Holman Highway), it will lead you back to Highway 1, but you won't want to miss the rest of Pacific Grove, so turn left at Forest Avenue. You will pass two large retirement residences, Canterbury Woods, operated by the Episcopal Homes Federation, and Forest Hill Manor, operated by the California-Nevada Methodist Homes, Inc. Continue down the hill to Lighthouse Avenue. This is the middle of the downtown shopping area, so find a parking place. There are no parking meters and, incidentally, no traffic lights downtown.

In 1880 the Methodist Bishop brought seed pods of eucalyptus trees from Australia and planted them in a double row along "Lighthouse Road." Some of the largest can be seen in front of the Post Office at Lighthouse and Congress Avenue.

The Pacific Grove Art Center is upstairs at 568 Lighthouse. They welcome visitors to their galleries and studios. Hours are 11:00 a.m. to 5 p.m., closed Sundays and Mondays.

The office of the Pacific Grove Chamber of Commerce at Forest and Central, a block below Lighthouse Avenue, is open from 9:00 a.m. to 5 p.m. Monday through Saturday. They will be happy to answer your questions and provide free brochures. For a dime you can buy an up-to-date street map of the entire Monterey Peninsula. You will find use for it later at Pebble Beach and in Carmel.

Only 177 museums throughout the United States and Canada have been accredited by the American Association of Museums; the Pacific Grove Museum of Natural History (across the street)

61

is one of thirteen in California to receive such accreditation. As long ago as 1935, the Association called this museum "the best of its size in the United States." It features monarch butterflies, marine and bird life, shells and Indian artifacts and has a native plant garden outdoors. Their relief map of Monterey Bay shows the great submarine canyon on its floor, 8,400 feet down, a gash deeper than the Grand Canyon. This tremendous chasm is one of the reasons why Monterey Bay has always been a fishing port. Upwelling waters bring nutrients to feed surface organisms which in turn provide food for the bay's fish. Museum hours are 10:00 a.m. to 5:00 p.m., closed Mondays. Admission is free. The Annual Wild Flower Show is held here in April and the Water Color Show in September.

When your feet get tired, Jewell Park is across the way. Or you might take the elevator to the Solarium atop Holman's Department Store. Enjoy some home-made cake or pie, a cup of coffee and a panoramic view of Monterey Bay. Holman's, which has served the Peninsula since 1891, was mentioned in "Cannery Row." John Steinbeck lived in Pacific Grove while doing research for "Cannery Row" and "Tortilla Flat."

You can play tennis all day for only fifty cents at the fine municipally-owned tennis courts up the hill behind the Community Center, 515 Junipero Avenue. There is playground equipment where the children can exhaust themselves before climbing back into the car. There are more tennis courts at the High School on Sunset Drive, available when school is not in session.

Washington Park is in the 900 block on Sinex Avenue and has complete picnic facilities and lots of trees, some with butterflies in them during the season. Beware of poison oak! The Little League Ball Park is here, too.

Seventeen Mile Drive Village at Sinex and Seventeen Mile Drive takes overnight campers, but space is limited so reserve early. Most of the motels are in the area around Asilomar Avenue and at the west end of Lighthouse Avenue, plus the two at Lovers Point.

Christmastime is special in Pacific Grove. The Assembly of God Church's Yuletide gift to the community is a wonderful Singing Christmas Tree with nightly performances the week before the holiday at the corner of Pine and Fountain Avenue. The whole city heralds the holiday season with an hour-long Santa Claus Parade the first Saturday in December. There are two outstanding areas where whole neighborhoods participate in outdoor decorating. One is Egan Avenue, just a few blocks up from Ocean View Boulevard. The other is "Candy Cane Lane" in Country Club Heights, a residential section just east of Forest Avenue. It is impossible to miss finding either place because they are so brightly lighted, and you can follow the parade of cars filled with wide-eyed children. The Fire Station on Pine Avenue always has a huge mechanical display. This firehouse welcomes visitors throughout the year. You'll see poinsettias the size of small trees in bloom in many Peninsula gardens this time of year, too.

Now that you have a whole roll of film of Pacific Grove, the "change-of-pace place" on the Monterey Peninsula, reload your camera. It's time to see Pebble Beach and the world-renowned Seventeen Mile Drive.

Picturesque Pebble Beach Golf Course.

4 ALONG SEVENTEEN MILE DRIVE, PEBBLE BEACH

Pebble Beach, where stately mansions are hidden in a verdant woodland and emerald fairways meet sapphire sea, is not a vast private residential park by accident. This greenbelt and majestic beach front of 8,400 acres were acquired in the early 1900's by its present owners, Del Monte Properties Company, under the leadership of the late Samuel F. B. Morse. The company has strict building codes governing the preservation of the area's beauty and bounty of nature. Guidelines for the 5,000-plus residents and for visitors have been established for the protection of native flora and fauna. Rules prohibit disturbing plant or animal life of any kind.

Dominating the dramatically laid out golf courses along a natural shoreline is Del Monte Lodge, world-famous hostelry, with its exclusive shops and fancy restaurants. Elite groups rule the social scene: Cypress Point Club, the Beach and Tennis Club, and Stillwater Yacht Club. Monterey Peninsula Country Club is on its own lovely knoll in "the Forest."

Golf can be enjoyed 365 days a year on the five championship courses: Pebble Beach, Cypress Point, Monterey Peninsula Country Club's shore and dunes courses, and Spyglass Hill. Pebble Beach, Spyglass, and Peter Hay Par 3 are open to the public. Major tournaments, such as the annual televised Bing Crosby Pro-Am, are played on three challenging courses within Pebble Beach's boundaries. The Pebble Beach Golf Links were chosen as the site of the 1972 U.S. Open.

Actor Clint Eastwood hosts a benefit Celebrity Tennis Tournament each July at the Beach and Tennis Club. Other recreational activities include equestrian events, rugby tournaments,

Photo by William C. Brooks

*A solitary cormorant surveys the
Pebble Beach shoreline.*

polo games, dog shows, regattas, and the Annual Gwen Graham Concours d'Elegance at Del Monte Lodge.

The exclusiveness of the area is apparent from first sighting; there are toll gates at each of the four entrances to this impressive retreat. Two are in Pacific Grove, one off Highway 1 and the other in Carmel. Residents have special license tags and come and go freely. Others must pay the three dollar entrance fee to see the world-acclaimed Seventeen Mile Drive. This gate fee is refundable if you plan to dine or stay at Del Monte Lodge. However, if you have a friend living in the Forest, phone him and ask him to call the security guard at the gate you intend to enter and you will be admitted free of charge. There is a well-marked bicycle route along the Drive, but bicyclists are required to get permits at the gate. Traffic laws are strictly enforced.

While you will be provided with a map of Seventeen Mile Drive showing all its points of interest along the yellow and orange painted line, do not stray too far from the designated route unless you have a complete map showing all roads, or you are sure to get lost and spend several hours trying to find your way out. The natives are friendly, though, so ask a pedestrian or knock on a door and the butler will gladly direct you.

From Pacific Grove, Seventeen Mile Drive follows the low white sand dunes and winds through exclusive residential sections past the showplace homes of some of America's most prominent citizens. You'll recognize their names on the front gateposts. The coastline changes from sandy dunes to jagged crags where ships have met their doom. Gnarled wind-blown Monterey cypress, which grow nowhere else in the world, offer unusual subject matter for camera buffs. Huge offshore rocks are populated by resting birds and lazy seals. Deer graze unconcernedly on lawns and golf greens. In the spring mother seals teach their babies to swim in the sheltered coves. A sudden geyser of water ejected from the ocean and then a visible dark hump denotes the presence of a

Photo by William C. Brooks

Clint Eastwood hosts Pebble Beach's
Celebrity Tennis Tournament.

passing whale in the spring or winter. Shaded picnic areas, over 100 miles of winding bridle trails, coves of quiet beauty and stretches of sandy shore abound at Pebble Beach.

As much as you have read or heard about this scenic wonderland, Seventeen Mile Drive rivals the Riviera and will still manage to exceed your expectations.

Basilica of Mission San Carlos Borromeo
del Rio Carmel.

5 BROWSING IN CARMEL-BY-THE-SEA

Indefinable Carmel-by-the-Sea, a captivating village that is really "by-the-Sea," is over the hill from Monterey. Carmel traces its heritage back to 1602 when Sebastian Vizcaino, after claiming Monterey for Spain, camped for a month near the Carmel River before sailing away to report his new discoveries to the King of Spain. Vizcaino named the sea and the land after the Carmelite monks who accompanied him on the voyage. Carmel was first settled in 1771 when Father Junipero Serra moved the Mission from Monterey to the more agreeable and arable setting of Carmel. Most of the settlers were Costanoan Indians.

Carmel Village proper, less than a square mile in size, didn't really burgeon until the late 19th century when it attracted a bonhomie of artists, authors and musicians. Their non-conformist way of life still prevails in the Carmel of today. The 1906 earth-quake left many of San Francisco's bohemians homeless. Poet George Sterling and novelist Mary Austin urged them to follow their lead to Carmel. Their small homes nestled in the forests and edged the sandy beaches. A group of citified professors built vacation cottages; one was David Starr Jordan who later became the first President of Stanford University.

This diversified group set a pattern for preserving their surroundings that is still rigidly observed. One of the township's first acts was to draw up an ordinance to protect the trees. Rather than felling a tree when the winding streets were laid out, the planners simply split the road to curve on both sides of the cherished tree. This puzzles yet delights visitors whose hometowns are concrete jungles. Showing utter disdain for progress, Carmel's pioneers decreed that there would be no street lights nor sidewalks in resi-

71

A prize-winning sand castle at Carmel Beach.

dential districts. Nowhere would there be high-rise buildings or neon signs, and commercial ventures would not sully the wide white beaches. Even AAA signs are custom-made to suit Carmel's rules.

Devendorf Plaza, the park off Ocean Avenue, was named for one of the town's first developers, J. Frank Devendorf. He and another entrepreneur, Frank H. Powers, acquired most of the acreage now known as Carmel in 1902. They leased and sold lots, preferably to people with artistic inclinations, for "a few dollars down and pay the balance when you can." Devendorf and Powers were interested in the arts and supported the Village's institutions like the Arts and Crafts Club formed in 1905. Among the distinguished writers associated with Carmel's early days were Jack London, Sinclair Lewis, Upton Sinclair and William Rose Benet. The unusual stone house and tower, "Tor House," which poet Robinson Jeffers helped build with his own hands, still stands overlooking Carmel Bay. Among the artists who appreciated the soul-searching solitude and stimulating beauty of Carmel were Armin Hansen, Arthur Hill Gilbert and Percy Gray.

Perry Newberry, a San Francisco newspaper artist, was one of the leading crusaders for preserving the city's unique independence. To keep progress from spoiling Carmel, he even suggested installing toll gates at its entrances! He felt that home mail deliveries were unnecessary, and to this day many villagers go daily to the friendly-staffed Post Office at 5th and Dolores to pick up their mail and exchange pleasantries with their fellow citizens. Reading the bulletin board outside the Post Office will give you an insight into their way of life, and reading a copy of the Carmel Pine Cone, an award-winning weekly newspaper, will, too. Because of city officials like Newberry, there are no honky-tonk strips of motels, gas stations and hot dog stands. In 1929 a zoning law decreed that business development should be forever subordinate to the residential character of the community.

Architectural emphasis has always been on individual expression. Even service stations are pleasing to the eye, some in the Spanish style, others with modern Oriental overtones. One thing is certain; there is no such thing as typical Carmel architecture. There are redwood board-and-bat homes, adobe dwellings, sturdy log cabins, Spanish villas with high-beamed ceilings and stone-flagged floors, ultra-contemporary mansions designed by world-famous architects, and then there are the Hansel and Gretel houses designed by Hugh Comstock. The latter have given Carmel its most lasting sobriquet, "A Storybook Hamlet." The Tuck Box tearoom on Dolores is an example of Comstock's "doll-house" period.

Hugh Comstock built a doll-sized house for his wife so she could display her hand-made "Otsy Totsy Dolls." Friends found the little house so "adorable" that Comstock was commissioned to build full-scale houses similar to it. These storybook-illustration homes are easily spotted along Carmel's winding, wooded streets. Comstock later perfected waterproof adobe bricks and built houses of these with redwood shakes and hewn timbers adding character.

Other architects responded to natural settings, designing seashore homes with a Mediterranean influence. English cottages, one with an imported thatched roof, and New England salt boxes stand side by side. Houses in the Village proper have no numbers, so their distinctive architecture is a great help in finding a friend's home for the first time.

Carmel's champagne-in-a-teacup atmosphere provides a welcome escape from the hasty pace of big cities. There is something about the scintillating sunshine, contrasting tender mists and downright fogs that makes even the retired shun the idle life. Carmel-by-the-Sea is a community of everyday and Sunday painters, poets, potters and putterers. In Carmel society you will find the attractive matron who checked your groceries in a gourmet market during the day sitting across from you at an elite dinner party in the evening.

This civilized, friendly community charms both young and old. Carmel Bay isn't safe for swimming, but it's great for surfing. Sunbathing and picnicking are favored pastimes. The Village's annual attractions range from kite-flying and sand-castle building to the glorious two-week long Bach Festival held in July at Sunset Center (San Carlos and 9th). This cultural complex has an assembly hall which seats 750, and various other meeting rooms accommodate 40 to 250 people. The studios here offer short-term instruction in various art forms for visitors.

Plan to spend a day in Carmel; if you don't, you will wish you had! Parking is a year-round problem. Instead of having to run back to your car and move it every hour or two, park several blocks north or south of Ocean Avenue where there are no limiting signs. Carmel is for walking and gawking, anyway.

Carmel-by-the-Sea is a city of serendipity. You have to do the exploring and discovering yourself. Window-shop along the main streets, of course, but wander back into the arcades and courts, too. Be sure to look up or you will "underlook" some of the most interesting places. Don't be reluctant about browsing; the shopkeepers love "lookers," and you will never be high-pressured into buying.

From the way-out boutiques to staid I. Magnin's, you'll find an extensive collection of clothing to fit any taste and any budget. Young Melissa at The Golden Door, Dolores and 7th, creates exquisite dresses for would-be princesses. If you have a Scottish surname, stop in the Scottish Shop on Ocean Avenue and look up your very own tartan. You'll find the best Irish fashions at Ferguson of Dublin and beautifully tailored English clothing at Derek Rayne or John Grissim, all on Ocean Avenue. The Robert John Shop at the Pine Inn has finely-made leather fashions, and for a lovingly hand-knit Scandinavian sweater, go to the Norway

Photo by Kevin Knox

*Father Serra's benevolent presence looks down
on Devendorf Plaza.*

House at Dolores and 5th. If your feet hurt, Anne Kalso from Copenhagen (Pantiles Court) developed the Earth Shoe to "re-create underfoot the natural terrain that now lies buried beneath the concrete of our cities."

Only in Carmel will you find the Christmas Shop where you can purchase delicate and fragile European ornaments all year long. Seals and Owls on Mission features authentic American Indian and Eskimo arts which you have probably never seen elsewhere. Little people will love the tiny Impulse Shoppe (Lincoln Lane) with its collection of miniatures of all kinds priced to please. There are several kitchen shops, including the Collector's Kitchen on Dolores and the French Chef Bazaar in the Doud Arcade, and for fine cutlery stop at Adam Fox on San Carlos where you can find the famed Swiss pocketknife and all sorts of fascinating weather instruments. Everything from place mats to laundry baskets can be bought at The Village Straw Shop on Lincoln. Enticing scents identify the many candle shops. Needlework of all kinds is in vogue once again. Intricate imported crewel or simple bookmark kits for beginning needlepointers can be found at the Danish Embroidery Shop on 6th. Antiques & Sew On, San Carlos and 7th, carries hundreds of European decorator trims and copies of antique doll kits for simple stuffing.

In the Doud Arcade, at the Nautilus, is the largest shell collection on the Peninsula and Nature's Jewel Box with displays of nature's handiwork including gems and minerals, stone carvings and custom jewelry. For one-of-a-kind jewelry, try Ruth Buol's Handcrafted Enamels, The House That Jack Built, Rice's Jewelry Shop or Studio 7 Jewelry Designers. For especially elegant jewelry from the world over, try Fourtaine's or Henri Corbat.

It will be hard to pass by bakery windows filled with flaky-fresh pigs' ears, alligator bread and gooey-good pastries and the candy stores with their home-made, hand-dipped chocolates and hand-pulled taffy. The Mediterranean Market, with its smelly imported cheeses and hanging salamis and all manner of irresistible food and drink, will make a sandwich for you just the way you want it.

Carmel has a choice of antique shops full of wonderful old treasures and objets d'art, including Luciano's, Parsons of Carmel, Carmel Clock Chalet, Crossroads, Love Antiques and many more.

Local craftsmen have found outlets here for their unique creations. Carmel Craft Studios and Laub's Carmel Craftsmen, both on Ocean Avenue, are good places to buy affordable, typical-Peninsula, take-home gifts.

Numerous fine art galleries show and sell the works of local artists and artisans and those of other artists from all over the world. You can watch weavers, potters and sculptors at work in their own studios. There are over fifty interesting galleries and studios, each as absorbing as the next. If you think you're not the gallery-browsing type, give it a try, anyway. You might be surprised and become so enthusiastic that you'll want to return tomorrow and finish your browsing. A small painting or sculpture will tuck in a suitcase and would be a worthwhile remembrance of your visit.

You would be hard pressed to find a restaurant in Carmel that does not serve good food; in fact, many have excellent food. From a great hamburger in the gruff atmosphere of the Rinky-Dink at Mission and 6th (when you can find it open; the owner is arbitrary) to the finest French cuisine in the elegant brocaded setting of The Marquis at San Carlos and 4th, there is a restaurant to suit every taste and every pocketbook.

The Carmel Butcher Shop has a fireplace fronting the sidewalk on Ocean Avenue so it's easy to find. They serve only USDA prime meats—mouth-watering steaks and prime rib on the dinner menu and tempting entrees, salads, sandwiches and sea foods for lunch. The Butcher Shop has a comfortable, homey atmosphere. Reservations are advised; this is one of Carmel's finest.

Each noble dish of Northern Italy and Tuscany served at Raffaello (Mission near Ocean) is a culinary masterpiece. In fact, folks say Raffaello has the best Italian food between Los Angeles and San Francisco. This is a small salon-type restaurant open for dinner only; it would be wise to make reservations several days ahead.

People call or write ahead for luncheon and dinner reservations at Simpson's (San Carlos and 5th), too. The menu includes Fresh Abalone Steak, Sole au Chablis, even Old-Fashioned Pot Roast. Only fresh vegetables are prepared, and the desserts are home-baked. Fragrant flowers always accent the dining room's mellow Williamsburg feeling.

There's a touch of Olde England at The Pump House, Junipero and 6th. Traditional roast beef and hearty English entrees like roast rack of lamb and steak and kidney pie are served by saucy wenches in 16th century costumes. Dinner hour starts at six. The Pump House also has an inexpensive tavern supper in their pub which opens at four.

You might rub elbows with the rich and famous at the restaurant and bar with the unlikely name, Hog's Breath Inn (San Carlos and 5th). Clint Eastwood is one of the owners. This small out-of-the way restaurant serves lunch and dinner and has become very popular with Peninsulans.

The best Chinese food is at the Tiki Hut, and for superior Scandinavian food and service, stop at Scandia, both on Ocean Avenue. It's worth standing in line for a sea food dinner at The Clam Box (Mission and 5th).

Unless you relish engrossing conversation in a cozy bar, night life is non-existent in Carmel. City law prohibits live entertainment in the hotels, restaurants and cocktail lounges.

There are few independently-owned hotels left, and Carmel has two of them. Guests used to arrive at the Pine Inn on Ocean Avenue by stage. This is Carmel's oldest inn and has been a part of the Village scene for three generations. The Victorian atmos-

Sunset-silhouetted Point Lobos across Carmel Bay.

phere is created by old prints, marble-topped tables, velvet flocked wallpaper and memorabilia of yesteryear. The Gazeboe is a new addition to this Carmel landmark, a glass-domed dining room in a garden setting with a giant chandelier to light the night. Luncheon and dinner are served daily, cocktails in the Red Parlor from 10:00 a.m.

La Playa Hotel at Camino Real and 8th, four blocks from the Village, has been a part of Carmel's tradition since the early part of the century. Oldyweds return year after year to this lovely old hotel where they spent their honeymoon. Newlyweds start their life together in the new Spanish Chapel. There are no waterfront hotels in Carmel, but La Playa is only two blocks from the beach so the dining room and many guest rooms have kaleidoscopic views of Carmel Bay and the ocean. Old-world decor is pointed up by conversation-piece furnishings throughout, and an Hispanic flavor is added by festive Mexican artworks. Nesting doves in huge wicker cages will please children in this family-favored hotel. In addition to breakfast, lunch and dinner in the picture-windowed Terrazzo Del Mar, cocktail lunches and suppers are served in La Taberna. La Playa's lobby shop specializes in carefully chosen, out-of-the-ordinary Mexican imports, reasonably priced.

Several years ago a Carmel radio station sponsored a contest to define Carmel. Here are some of the entries:

Carmel is untamed domesticity.
Carmel is why other villages turn green.
Carmel is the place that puts the heart in hearthstone.
Carmel is where you'll never find neon in an eon.
Carmel is quaint like other places ain't.
Carmel is "Bach" to the old drawing board.
Carmel is the pit stop in the human race.
Carmel is T-bone to "browser."

81

Carmel is "Bach"-ward oh, time, in thy flight.
Carmel is a sand castle come to life.
Carmel is where there's a kook in every nook and a granny in every cranny!

Carmel is indescribable! Perhaps by now you have formulated your own definition for this "charming-quaint-enchanting-story-book-fairytale" village by the sea.

You will want to take Carmel's Scenic Road along the tree-bordered bay. Turn left at the foot of Ocean Avenue. Drive slowly; this is a narrow, twisting street with a fine view of the bay and a look at varied architecture. After rounding the Carmel River lagoon, turn left on Carmelo Street, then right on 15th Avenue, which will lead you to the Mission, Basilica of Mission San Carlos Borromeo del Rio Carmel.

Originally built in 1771, this Mission was Father Junipero Serra's headquarters until his death in 1784. He is buried at the foot of the present altar. The first adobe church was replaced by a larger stone edifice in 1797 under the direction of Father Lasuen. In 1834 the Mexican Government, then ruling California, ordered the secularization of the Missions. The Franciscan Fathers were sent back to Spain, and Carmel Mission, without their guidance, was abandoned in 1836. The Indians, who tended its corrals, vast granging lands for sheep and cattle, and its farming acreage, were left homeless and helpless and became scattered throughout the territory.

The first steps toward restoration of this Mission took place under Father Ramon Mestres in 1924. Harry Downie, renowned authority on California Mission architecture and reconstruction and present curator, along with Father Michael D. O'Connell, took over and completed the task. Since 1933 the Carmel Mission has been the parish church.

You can feel the stateliness of the Mission's early days interwoven with the Peninsula's past the moment you push open the bare wooden door that leads to a courtyard reminiscent of Spanish-Colonial times. The imposing stone church with its tower dome is surrounded by well-kept gardens. There are two museums on the grounds whose array of practical and religious treasures reveal the hardy, industrious and austere life style of Father Serra and the Franciscan monks who were his contemporaries. The kitchen and the tiny modest room where Father Serra slept have been reproduced.

In 1960 Pope John XXIII elevated Mission San Carlos Borromeo del Rio Carmel to the highly dignified rank of Basilica, one of only eleven churches so designated in the United States and one of only two Basilicas in the western states.

Photo by Julian P. Graham

Pastoral Carmel Valley.

6 THROUGH CARMEL VALLEY

Many Indian artifacts have been found on Carmel Valley ranches. Long ago tribes moved up and down the valley, to and from the coast according to the seasons. Early settlers acquired their acreage through Mexican and Spanish land grants. The 64,000 verdant acres of this unincorporated pastoral valley, stretching fourteen miles east of Carmel, are surrounded by the rugged Santa Lucia Mountains to the south and the high ridge of the Peninsula to the north. The 6,000 residents live in homes varying from the unpretentious to the pretentious. Some sprawl graciously along the Carmel River banks while others hang by their chimneys on the hillsides. Carmel Valley's climate is warmer than elsewhere on the Peninsula, so the landscape is punctuated with resorts, restaurants, theaters and recreational facilities, some public, others posh and private. There are large orchards and truck gardens, dude and cattle ranches. The hotels and motels are more than just places to stay overnight; all offer a variety of interesting activities.

The Carmel River flows thirty miles northwest through the coastal ranges to south of Carmel. Steelhead season opens in mid-November and runs through February. Whether or not fishing is good depends on rainfall and the amount of water released by Los Padres and San Clemente Dams upstream. If you are over sixteen, you will need a license for fresh-water fishing.

Boar hunting is not for beginners. Russian wild boars were brought to this country from the Ukrainian Mountains in 1919 to a hunting preserve on the border of North Carolina and Tennessee. Thirteen boars were shipped to Monterey County in 1924.

They mated with runaway domesticated swine, and hundreds now roam the inaccessible regions of the Santa Lucia Mountains. The average boar killed weighs 250 pounds. They are dangerous and fast. Special wild boar hunts are conducted in season, also deer and mountain lion hunts in the Santa Lucias.

Neighboring shopping areas at the mouth of the Valley, Carmel Rancho Center, and Carmel Center, are connected by a road at the rear. The Hatchcover Steak House in Carmel Rancho Center serves excellent lunches and dinners on real hatchcover tables in a friendly informal atmosphere. They have live contemporary music in the bar Wednesday through Saturday evenings. If you plan to picnic in the Valley, buy the fixings in one of the super markets. Or you might go to the far end of Carmel Center's arcade, with its two huge metal-sculptured fountains, and buy a complete picnic lunch to go at Yosef's Delicatessen.

The entrance to the Valley is a few miles south of Carmel to the east of Highway 1, so let's discover Carmel Valley. . .

Rancho Cañada Golf Club, a mile east, has two side-by-side public courses that wind back and forth over five bridges across the Carmel River, complete clubhouse facilities and a fine pro shop. Even if you're not a golfer, you can join the cleat crowd for lunch. The bar and dining room look out over the beautiful greens, the river and the rolling tree-studded hills. A prime rib and cracked crab buffet is served Fridays only.

There are two adult communities, Del Mesa Carmel and Hacienda Carmel, and a retirement community, Carmel Valley Manor, operated by Northern California Congregational Homes, Inc., before you reach mid-valley.

Drive through the grounds of the beautiful Quail Lodge at Carmel Valley Golf and Country Club (private). It is one of three resort hotels in California given the coveted rating of "Outstanding" by AAA. Its award-winning architecture is worth seeing, a little expensive to stay, though. Quail Lodge does have a special package for tennis buffs or golfers that is modestly priced, however.

The unparalleled Thunderbird Bookshop is at Valley Hills Shopping Center. While you are enjoying lunch or a light supper, you can read one of over 50,000 books offered for sale and return it to the shelf when you have finished eating. Where else but on the Monterey Peninsula? Before leaving Valley Hills, get the feel of Carmel Valley by reading the notices posted on the sides of the buildings.

There are several stands along the way, including Wolters Hacienda Market, where you can buy fresh fruits and vegetables grown in the Valley. The great piles of bright orange pumpkins are a joy to see in October.

Turning right at Schulte Road will lead first to Riverside Park and then to Saddle Mountain Recreation Park beyond. The Riverside Campground (3.7 acres), about 3/4 mile in, is open year-round. There are twenty trailer sites (all up to 32 feet limit) and fifteen tent sites with full facilities, recreation room and a small store. You may picnic during the day here, too.

Saddle Mountain Recreation Park is a mile in from Carmel Valley Road and has something for everyone in the family. This 100-acre park includes a heated pool with adjacent wading pool, snack bar, recreation hall with pool tables, juke box and room for private evening parties. Outdoor games include ping pong, volley ball, badminton, horseshoes, and a children's playground. All these facilities are open from April through October. Saddle Mountain takes campers all year-round. There are fifty campsites with full facilities for sleeping bags, tents, trailers or recreational vehicles. A 3½ mile hiking trail will take you to an elevation of 1,000 feet for a superb view of Moss Landing, the Santa Cruz Mountains and Los Padres Forest.

Visit the Carmel Valley Begonia Gardens if you're a green-thumber or just have a fondness for beautiful begonias.

Beyond Carmel Valley Village.

The Mid-Valley Shopping Center has complete facilities. If you have changed your mind about picnicking, there is a super market here.

The proprietors of the Country Store at the friendly Farm Center love sightseers as well as spenders and are very knowledgeable about Carmel Valley. There is a complete Western Store, including a bigger-than-life replica of a horse. Lift your little ones up for a pretend ride on "Charlie." The Paddock Room downstairs stocks elegant English riding clothes; ladies will love the Tumbleweed Dress Shop; and the Tack Shop out back houses a complete line of Western and English tack. While you're out there, notice the photogenic old sand plant across the road. It looks as if it might collapse at any moment, but it is still operated whenever the owner has need for sand.

The Korean Buddhist Temple, Sambosa (Three Treasures), is just west of the Farm Center off Robinson Canyon Road. It is situated on 7½ acres facing the gently flowing river with serene mountains as a background, a setting similar to that of its sister temple in Seoul, Korea. The natural wood structure is Oriental in theme and spirit, gracefully blending East and West. The public is invited to attend regular Sunday services at 11:00 a.m.

If you packed that picnic lunch, turn toward the Carmel River, about a mile ahead on Rancho Fiesta Road. There is a quiet, grassy spot on the river bank where localites have picnicked for many years.

Los Laureles Grade goes over the tops of the mountains to the north. This scenic drive ends up on State Highway 68 leading to Salinas.

White Oaks Theater is leased by Hidden Valley Music Seminar. Hidden Valley was organized to bring young artists, students and teachers together in the most productive environment possible. Five-week seminars are held during the summer to train youngsters for the professional world of music. The new dormitory behind the theater will accommodate eighty students. Musicals are presented at White Oaks and at Sunset Center in Carmel. Their Children's Theater Division brings live professional productions into classrooms throughout the Monterey Peninsula.

The "Madonna of the Village," between White Oaks and the Post Office complex, spreads joy, peace and love throughout "the Village." There are many stores to explore. Be sure to include Giuseppe's Work Bench where handmade jewelry is designed, the delightful In and Outdoor Shop, the Monterey Pottery Shop, and the Carmel Valley Gallery and Craft Center. Everyone who loves food ends up at Carmel Valley Market where they stock everything from reindeer meatballs to just plain tuna fish, among thousands of unusual delicacies, including beer from twelve countries, and twelve different cabernets.

Rosie's Cracker Barrel on the far side of the Esquiline Road bridge has been an institution since 1939. Its proprietor, William Irwin Henry, got his nickname "Rosie" when he played ball in the Abalone League because of his once-red hair and ruddy complexion. He spent nine years as Carmel Valley's Postmaster. Rosie's name is emblazoned on a brass plaque on his original cracker barrel, now converted into an upholstered seat. Rosie might be pumping gas at the station next door, serving beer in the bar, waiting on a customer in the store or just loafing on a bench in the sunshine. His establishment has long been a local gathering place. There are weather-beaten tables and benches for customers. The sign on the side of the building, made by the local kids, says "Robles Del Rio Country Club."

There are a number of excellent restaurants in and near the Village. Will's Fargo with its nostalgic gaslight atmosphere lets the diner choose his own steak and have it broiled to order. The lamb chops and broiled lobster are great, too. Top it all off with Carmel Valley Walnut Pie. Will's is closed January through March, however. Plaza Linda serves great chili relleno, and Blan-

90

quita's has tasty Mexican lunches and dinners, too. The Little European Restaurant's food is authentic and good. The Buckeye has a rustic atmosphere and a friendly crowd with live entertainment in the bar some evenings. Their specialty is early California cuisine, including prime rib dinners and home-made desserts like lingonberry cobbler in season. Next door is the Carriage House with a cozy atmosphere and continental dinners.

Near the Village is a normally fog-free 1,800 foot airstrip suitable for single and light twin-engine planes.

Beyond the Village, Carmel Valley Road will take you to the Comsat (Communications Satellite) Earth Station near Jamesburg, about ten miles. The "dish" antenna stands taller than a ten-story building. Visitors may take guided tours on Saturdays and Sundays between 1:00 and 3:00 p.m. A brief movie concerning the operation of the Station is shown, then a technician explains the complicated electronic equipment, how the signal is received from and transmitted to the satellite. If you are lucky, you might see a Sunday football game in the fall. The Earth Station is not classified, and you may take pictures. Call ahead (659-2293) if you plan to visit; sometimes equipment is installed over a weekend and visitors are barred.

Turning south on Cachagua Road for about ten miles will lead you to the turnoff to Prince's Camp and Los Padres Dam. Pass through Prince's Camp, a community of mostly trailer homes clustered around a busy bar and a small store with higher-than-usual prices. Park your car near the Ranger Station and then walk in to Los Padres Reservoir, owned by the California-American Water Co. There is a U.S. Forest Service Park here. Trout fishing is good in season, but no power boats are allowed on the lake, just self-propelled. It is about half a mile on a dirt road to the actual dam. This park is crowded in the summertime and on sunny weekends. However, hiking is a back-to-nature experience. This is one of the starting points to the profusion of trails throughout the

Los Padres Forest, and you must sign in at the Ranger Station if you intend to hike into the wilderness.

Farther along Cachagua Road is the turn-off to China Camp and Tassajara Hot Springs (Tassajara Road). China Camp near Chews Ridge has full facilities for overnight camping and a Ranger Station. Beyond here the road is more difficult to drive.

Tassajara Hot Springs were known to the Indians and later to the Spaniards for their chalybeate qualities. The name comes from the Spanish-American word "tasajera," meaning "a place where meat is cut in strips and hung in the sun to dry." From 1904 on it became a fashionable retreat with a large brownstone hotel, which burned in 1949, and rustic buildings and bath houses along Arroyo Seco Creek. For a distance of 200 yards, seventeen hot mineral springs issue from the mountainside at a temperature of 140-150° F. The water contains sulphur, sodium, magnesia, iron and phosphate. These springs are deep in an isolated valley amid the lofty Santa Lucia peaks. The road into the 480-acre property was built in the 1880's by Chinese labor. In those days a stagecoach left Salinas at 6:00 a.m. and arrived at Tassajara at 6:30 p.m., a distance of 53 miles. While the road is much improved, it is still an hour and a half drive from Carmel Valley Village. It is winding, scenic and somewhat precipitous, definitely a low-gear journey. In 1967 the Zen Center of San Francisco purchased Tassajara Hot Springs Resort, and it is now headquarters for Zen study and training in North America. New buildings have been added, and the mineral baths are being developed in the Japanese tradition. In the summertime visitors are welcome during daylight hours. For a dollar or two you can picnic and enjoy the baths. Their dining room is open to overnight guests only and is highly recommended. Emphasis is on simple vegetarian food. Make overnight reservations early. Tassajara is closed to the public during the winter months when the Center is used only for student training.

7 EXPANDING SEASIDE

Dr. John L. D. Roberts came to the Monterey Peninsula in 1887 with only a new medical certificate from New York University's Medical School and a single old silver dollar in his pocket. He became a familiar figure making house calls on horseback along the Big Sur coast, all the while charting the wilderness and dreaming of the day when there would be a highway. He saw that dream realized in 1937 when Highway 1 was dedicated. Dr. Roberts bought a 160-acre ranch, on what is now Seaside and Sand City, from his uncle for $5,000 and filed a butcher paper map as his claim to the title. Within a year he had paid for the land in full, had money in the bank, owned his own home and had 1,000 additional lots to sell.

In 1897 this remarkable man made a five-day trip on foot from San Luis Obispo to Monterey and mapped the rugged country in between. Eighteen years later he stood before the California legislature showing colored slides on a bedsheet and describing this magnificent land he loved so much. As a result, the State earmarked $1½ million for building a highway.

Dr. Roberts founded the Seaside Post Office in 1890, and Seaside was born. He, and his wife later, acted as Postmaster for 42 years. In the twenty years the Doctor served on the Monterey County Board of Supervisors, four of them as Chairman, he never missed a meeting. He saw that the Presidio of Monterey was enlarged and rebuilt in 1902 and pioneered the building of Highway 1 between Monterey and Castroville. A fitting memorial to this man of vision is Roberts Lake in Seaside where youngsters of all ages enjoy remote-control boating.

*Seaside's City Complex, designed
by Edward Durell Stone.*

Seaside's slogan is: "Seaside means business!" It is the fastest growing residential and commercial community on the Monterey Peninsula with a population nearing 40,000, five times its pre-war size. The city has made great strides in overcoming its early image of a wide-open frontier town. Seaside grew haphazardly until its incorporation in 1954. Speculators took their money and moved on, leaving the land little improved. Squatters built shacks and settled in the sand dunes and sagebrush and didn't bother to plant trees. During depression years lots sold for as little as one dollar. The San Francisco Chronicle offered free lots in Seaside as a come-on for new subscribers, few of whom ever settled there. With the start of World War II and the establishment of the huge Fort Ord complex, land values rose. Since then an extensive urban renewal program has helped to replace substandard homes with hundreds of new homes in the growing residential areas overlooking the Peninsula skyline and Monterey Bay. Many military and civilian personnel from Fort Ord and the Naval Postgraduate School make their homes here. The citizens of Seaside are proud of their city's international character; nearly every race in the world is represented among its residents.

The Seaside City Hall, on a 5⅓-acre site at 440 Harcourt Avenue, was designed by world-renowned architect Edward Durell Stone. It consists of three main elements, Council chamber, administrative offices and Police Department. The total area within the building is 19,100 square feet. A continuous and changing showing of art works is on display here. Hours are 8:00 a.m. to 5:00 p.m., closed Saturdays and Sundays.

Gateway Center, 1664 Hilby Avenue, is a remarkable community project, started by a small group of parents motivated by a common aim—to do something for their mentally handicapped children. From this humble beginning, assisted by a generous donation from the Bing Crosby Foundation, Gateway Center grew and is now operated by the California State Departments of

*Monterey Peninsula Buddhist Temple, Seaside,
expresses classic Oriental beauty.*

Mental Hygiene and Education and is only one of four in the state offering such a child development program.

The Monterey Peninsula Buddhist Temple at 1155 Noche Buena is an unexpected and appreciated sight. A latticed gate leads into this large compound of Oriental beauty with its classic gardens, water falling into a pond of goldfish and the glass-sided buildings beyond. English-speaking services are held Sundays at 10:15 a.m. Tours of the Temple may be arranged by calling 394-0119. First, second and third generation Japanese (Isei, Nisei and Sansei) sponsor the two-day Obon Festival at the Monterey Fairgrounds in July, featuring Japanese food, formalized dancing, flower arranging, tea ceremonies and cultural displays. An Annual Bonsai Show is also held at the Buddhist Temple in May.

Urban Redevelopment Programs have made Seaside a forerunner for cities of its size. Among four renewal projects is the Monterey Peninsula Auto Center, a new concept in new-car shopping. It is an eight-dealer complex built around meandering pedestrian malls.

An eight-foot wide pedestrian-equestrian-bicycle trail starts at the northern edge of Seaside's city limits and goes to the Fort Ord main gate near Gigling Road where there is a vista point. Eventually this $94,000 trail will lead all the way to Marina and will be the longest in the State and the first to be built next to a freeway.

The rolling surf at Asilomar State Beach.

8 CLOSE-BY COMMUNITIES

DEL REY OAKS

In a sun pocket sandwiched between Monterey and Seaside, nestled in a grove of oak trees, is the quiet residential community of Del Rey Oaks. Since its incorporation in 1953, the 2,000 residents have carefully preserved the family quality of Del Rey Oaks. All but four lots are zoned for single-family homes. In the middle of the 386 wooded acres, on the floor of Canyon Del Rey, is a 34-acre park. The stream running through the canyon feeds Laguna Grande and Roberts Lake. Facilities include a recreation building, golf driving range, tennis courts and a ball field, all built with aid from the Bing Crosby Youth Fund.

SAND CITY

Sand City is located in the rolling dunes across the railroad tracks from Seaside. It has the distinction of being the second smallest incorporated city in the State and is described as "a mile wide and a mile-and-a-half long." Sand City has a residential population of approximately 500, but nearly 2,000 workers are employed in its commercial and light industrial establishments.

FORT ORD

Fort Ord was named after Major General Edward Otho Cresap Ord, a famed Indian fighter who served in the early days as a Lieutenant under General Fremont, commanded the first U.S. Army Garrison at the present site of the Presidio of Monterey and later distinguished himself as a combat officer in the Civil War.

In 1917 the Federal Government acquired 15,324 acres near the present East Garrison. It was known as Gigling Reservation,

*Live melodramas are still presented
at California's First Theatre.*

named after a German family who once lived in the area; Gigling Road still bears their name. Few improvements were made until 1933. More than 20,000 acres were added in 1940, and Camp Ord became Fort Ord. Additional land has been acquired since; now Fort Ord encompasses 28,500 acres. During World War II it was a staging and training area averaging about 35,000 troops. At one time there were more than 50,000.

Today the U.S. Army Training Center, Infantry, Fort Ord, has four training brigades and one Committee Group with about 42,000 personnel. There are more than 22,000 military dependents and an estimated 16,500 retired military and their dependents from all services supported by Fort Ord's facilities. Over 2,000 civilians are employed here.

Fort Ord's facilities include 4 service clubs, 6 libraries, 6 theaters, 8 craft shops, 33 exchanges, 6 indoor and 46 outdoor sports facilities, 11 chapels and a new 8-story 440-bed hospital which you can see on the skyline. If you are curious about the red flags flying on the bayside of the highway, it means the infantrymen are practicing on the target ranges.

MARINA

In 1915 William Locke Paddon, a San Francisco land promoter, bought 1,500 desolate acres. He was the only one who had faith in the future of Marina. Today there are many who wish they could have purchased property for twenty dollars an acre as Paddon did. The little undeveloped land left in Marina now sells for hundreds of times that amount. For years this sandy land was devoted to the cultivation of peas and potatoes. Marina still retains a rural atmosphere although the only thing still the same today is the railroad. In the late fifties subdivisions grew, and now there are acres of homes to the east of the highway which house a population of 12,000. Marina, the gateway to the Monterey Peninsula, is a "bedroom community" and the home of many military personnel attached to Fort Ord. If you brought your trail bike, Marina has a track in the sand dunes. Children will enjoy Marina's Annual Kids' Day held in April.

A few miles north of Marina is Salinas River State Beach in the huge sand dunes. The park is undeveloped but you can play in the dunes and on the beach. The frontage extends almost to Moss Landing. To reach it, take Mulligan Hill Road, off Molera Road.

9 CASTROVILLE, THE ARTICHOKE CAPITAL

Juan Bautista Castro, who was born in Monterey in 1835, inherited almost 40,000 acres from his wealthy and distinguished family. His father, Simeon C. Castro, was the first Alcalde (Mayor) of Monterey, and his mother was the sister of California's last Governor under Mexican rule. Young Castro realized that the area's future depended on attracting and encouraging new settlers. He subdivided his land into large ranches and donated property for a townsite, which he named "Castroville." By 1875 this second oldest town in Monterey County was flourishing with a population of 1,000. The Southern Pacific had a right-of-way and passengers ate a hurried lunch at the new hotel while the train's crew changed. The county's first hospital was built, and Wells Fargo established an office. The new brewery spawned thirteen saloons. Don Juan Bautista, as he was known, presided over the community and was among the last of the California Dons. Unwise investments left him nearly penniless. He endured failing health in his waning years and died in 1915. There is a simple gravesite in the small cemetery which he donated to the town many years before.

When the Southern Pacific moved its main line east to Salinas, Castroville was nearly forgotten. The population dwindled to only a few hundred. Even so, some Spanish land grant holders in the area did not sell out. Descendants of the Cooper and Molera families still own and operate portions of original grants. At the turn of the century most of the rich acreage was planted in potatoes and wheat, but it was a thistle that saved Castroville. Because of the artichoke, the population now tops 3,000.

The first artichokes in America were planted by the French

The thistle that saved Castroville.

in Louisiana and Florida and by the Spanish in California. They are native to North Africa and the Mediterranean region. Italian immigrants brought them to Half Moon Bay, north of the Monterey Peninsula. Flat farmland was scarce there and in the 1920's these farmers began to buy and lease as much land as possible at Castroville.

A weather-beaten sign spans Castroville's main street proclaiming it "The Artichoke Center of the World." Actually it exaggerates; Italy, France and Spain out-produce Castroville, but it can claim fame as "the artichoke heart" of the United States. About 10,000 acres are devoted to the cultivation of artichokes, and Castroville produced 85% of the country's crop. Most of the growers are Italian, and the field and plant workers are Mexican-American. Seventy-five percent of the crop is shipped fresh throughout the country. Speed is the secret of successfully trimming and quick-freezing this delicate vegetable. The rest of the crop is processed in several plants. Annually six million jars of marinated artichokes are shipped out of Castroville. Only a few hours elapse between the time they are picked from the dewy fields in the morning until they are packed into jars and stored in the warehouses. The recipe for the spicy oil marinade has been handed down from generation to generation by Italian families.

Planting takes place in the summer and fall. Artichokes produce within six months, depending upon sunshine and rain. From then on they are picked every five to ten days and are normally through producing by May. With a pruning process called "stumping," the plants will bear again within 100 days. Without man's help, artichokes would be available only four months of the year. New planting takes place every seven years.

Roadside stands have morning-picked artichokes year-round and fresh mushrooms, too. Some will ship artichokes anywhere for you, and all have free recipes for preparing them in various ways.

The Annual Artichoke Festival is held in Castroville on a September weekend. Everyone is welcome at the community dinner Friday evening, pancake breakfast, parade and coronation ball for the Artichoke Queen on Saturday and chicken and artichoke barbecue Sunday.

If you turn left at Molera Road just before reaching the junction of Highway 1 and Highway 156, you can drive through the picturesque, precision-planted artichoke fields. It is a good two-lane paved road with little traffic leading to the edge of Moss Landing. While this is an interesting drive, you will miss everyone's favorite "thistle stop," the Giant Artichoke, where there is a wine- and cheese-tasting room, also an array of fresh fruits and vegetables in unusual display bins, a gift shop and a restaurant that serves artichokes every imaginable way, just plain boiled, in salad, in cake or bread, marinated or french-fried. Buy some french-fried artichokes to go; they're delicious!

The original hotel burned in 1925 and was replaced with the Franco Hotel. It has only ten rooms, a bar and a dining room and lots of old country atmosphere. Italian food, prepared the way it should be, is served along with artichokes, of course. If you need to make up a Rotary meeting, do it at the Franco Hotel Friday noon. This will be like no other meeting you have attended, farmers in working clothes and great conversation.

IO MOSS LANDING, THE SNUG HARBOR

Shortly before the Civil War, Paul Lezere, a Frenchman, purchased 300 acres from the State for $300 and called it "City of St. Paul." This land eventually became the salt works north of Elkhorn Slough, which you can visit and which has been in operation at Moss Landing since the middle of the 19th century. Salt water is drawn into ponds and passes through five evaporating beds before it becomes pure salt. The pinky-white mountain of salt is surrounded by tidepools and swamps which are a nesting ground for many species of birds and a favorite spot for bird-watchers. No power boats are allowed in the winding canals of the Slough, just canoes, kayaks and rowboats. Some of the salt ponds are now being used for raising brine shrimp for bait.

Lezere installed a ferry across Elkhorn Slough, now spanned by the highway bridge. A few people bought lots, but none ever built homes, so he sold his land in 1871 to Cato Vierra, a native of the Portuguese-owned Azores, who replaced the ferry with a toll bridge. Members of the same Vierra family live near the original land.

Captain Charles Moss, a Texan with foresight and determination, arrived about this time. He envisioned an opportunity to develop the port to handle the large shipments of grain grown in the Pajaro and Salinas Valleys. Together Moss and Vierra built a wharf, and the first ship to sail out of the new port carried 100 tons of wheat which hired men had to carry on their backs through waist-deep water, load on surf boats and transfer to the ship. Soon the port became known as "Moss's Landing," later shortened to "Moss Landing." Steamers stopped regularly carrying dairy products, cured meats and hides to San Francisco. On return trips

Photo by Roy-Ami Hamlin

Antique cars parked at new "Old Moss Landing."

they brought early settlers to the two agricultural valleys. In 1874 the Southern Pacific line was extended to Watsonville and slough traffic diminished, although barge traffic continued for another fifteen years. Captain Moss left his namesake for San Francisco with a quarter of a million dollars. Amid the early-day photographs hanging on the walls of the tiny renovated Moss Landing Post Office is a sign offering a reward of five dollars for a picture of Captain Moss.

Between 1917 and 1927, folks didn't have to ask directions to Moss Landing; they followed their noses! That was the time when a whaling station was established on the island and as many as five whales a week were hauled in. During prohibition Moss Landing was also a haven for rum-runners. The whales departed for better waters, and the sardines arrived. After the depression Moss Landing's economy soared as purse seiners brought in hundreds of tons of sardines nightly. The sardines disappeared in the middle forties, as they did at Monterey, leaving the district desperate for funds. Sometimes there was barely enough to pay utility bills.

The Army Corps of Engineers built the channel in 1946. It is 200 feet wide with a 15 feet deep entrance and runs from the sand dunes at the tip of Monterey Bay's submarine canyon to the inner harbor. The canyon is at the seaward end of the entrance to the channel and has a calming effect on adjacent waters even during roughest storms. Moss Landing's T-shaped harbor has long been considered the safest refuge between Los Angeles and San Francisco. Skippers say they can "tie their boats with a shoe-string."

While their establishment improved district finances, Moss Landing's industries are sometimes lauded and sometimes lamented. Along Highway 1, parallel to the mooring basin, are two giant industries. The Pacific Gas and Electric Company's steam generating plant, dubbed "Mighty Moss," looks like a lit-up battleship at night from across the Bay. By a very complex operation, Kaiser Refractories manufactures basic refractory brick used in high-temperature furnaces in the steel, glass and cement industries. Since their establishment, however, Moss Landing's citizens, who now number 650, have reconsidered their district's industrial future. Seriously concerned about pollution of all kinds, they have set up rigid restrictions for industries wanting to locate here. Moss Landing is not likely to become a huge industrial complex; boats are Moss Landing's business. More than three hundred fishing boats are moored in the basin during off-season months. Each morning dozens puff out in search of salmon, tuna, albacore and other large fish. On the west side of the highway is Elkhorn Yacht Club where handsome sailboats and cruisers are tied up.

The tombstones in the little old cemetery to the left as you approach Moss Landing are fascinating reading, a look into the town's lively past.

The freshest organically grown fruits and vegetables in these parts are at Johnny Boys on the highway.

Turn down Moss Landing Road and plan to spend a few hours. You can find anything from buttons to bureaus in this antique browsers' paradise. Moss Landing currently has seventeen antique shops. Pirate Cove Flea Market has forty shops of various kinds under one roof, open every day in the summer and Thursday through Sunday in the winter. That's a one-way bridge on Sandholt Road leading to the island. You'll just have to back across it after you have visited Pirate Cove because the natives are determined to keep it. Who else has a one-way bridge?

Whatever you're looking for, you will probably find it in one of Moss Landing's charming shops with delightful names like Déjà Vu, Clowns Alley, 1897 or Thereabouts, Tin Whale, Now and Then or Ye Olde Sail Shoppe. All the stores in town have free maps of Moss Landing and vicinity, courtesy of the Chamber of Commerce, so pick one up at your first stop.

Jomar & Associates next to the Post Office is a stained glass workshop specializing in custom-designed lamps, windows and ornaments, each an original masterpiece. They also repair old pieces. You'll find old and new pianos, organs and phonographs, even old player rolls, at The Old Music Maker; beautiful custom-made leather goods at the Leather Bag; collectibles for gentlemen and railroadiana at The Country Peddler; Mother Lode jewelry at The Purple Pelican; a marvelous collection of antique buttons at the Stagecoach; oriental art and furniture at The Lotus House; quick pastel portraits at Portraits by Koosje; and "everything from toys to rain-proof aprons" at the Souvenir Shop.

Moss Landing owes much of its changing character to Roy-Ami Hamlin, portrait painter, antique dealer and professional interior designer, who moved here from Monterey. You have seen some of his fine work at the Sardine Factory and Flora's on Cannery Row in Monterey, at the Butcher Shop in Carmel and at Will's Fargo in Carmel Valley. Hamlin owns much of the property at the foot of the bridge, including the old Standard Oil bulk plant which has been converted into an antique emporium. Under his guidance other old buildings are being renovated and the town businesses, though small, are colorful and interesting.

In 1965 five state colleges (San Jose, San Francisco, Sacramento, Fresno and Hayward) purchased the former Palmer Beaudette Foundation laboratory and established a major scientific center, Moss Landing Marine Laboratories, on Sandholt Road. Graduate students study marine biology, oceanography and related subjects hoping to bridge the gap between industrial and conservation interests. Open house is held at the Laboratories in May.

If you decide to picnic on the beach or if you're going fishing, pick up barbecued ribs, chicken or beef to go, like the fishermen do, at the Lucky Rib Hut next to the Post Office. There is no inside seating, but you can lean against the hitching rail outside.

Moss Landing's business is boats.

Moss Landing has two unusual restaurants, both right on the Bay overlooking the harbor and its attendant activities. Drive north across the bridge. You can't miss Skipper's; it's painted passionate purple and is on the site where Cato Vierra built his first home. Skipper's is a family affair, serving breakfast and lunch, and specializing in local sea foods and chowder. If you are fond of fresh home-baked rhubarb pie, order it here.

Genovese's Harbor Inn nearby, also family-owned and operated, serves sea food with an Italian flair. Their Calameri (squid) is excellent. For a memorable experience, spend Saturday night at the Harbor Inn and dance to "We Three," a combo right out of the fifties. These near-senior citizens have been playing here for over fifteen years. Sip Tuaca (Italian coffee with rum) and soak up old-world atmosphere. You will never feel like a stranger at the Harbor Inn, and you will come away feeling like there is hope for all of us.

Moss Landing has all kinds of fishing, from party boats or small boats, from the docks, from the shore inside the harbor or from the jetties. Shore fishing is good at the mouth of the Pajaro River at Zmudowski State Beach (156 acres). This is a day-use park for swimming, picnicking and fishing. Fishing licenses are available at M. L. Liquors. (Where else?) Be a conservationist; instead of poking in tidepools for bait, buy it at the bait shack. You can dig clams in the Slough or at Zmudowski Beach down Giberson Road. Be careful; the tide and undertow are tricky. You can camp overnight unofficially near the beach off Jetty Road, but facilities are primitive.

Little Baja on the highway is packed with Mexican imports. You have never seen so many clay pots of all sizes and shapes before and, of course, they have the usual paintings on velvet and sundry bric-a-brac. However, if you have been wanting to order some custom-made wrought iron work, this is the place to do it inexpensively. Children will enjoy seeing the hundreds of birds for sale in their aviary out back.

By now you have fallen in love with Moss Landing and the friendly folks who live here, so come back for their Annual Festival and Fish Fry in August or their Shark Derby in late May and early June or join in the fun at the community Hallowe'en Parade and Party.

II SIGHTSEEING TOURS

POINT LOBOS

Point Lobos State Reserve is south of Carmel off Highway 1. This is a primitive paradise and a nature lover's dream. Hours are 9:00 a.m. to 7:00 p.m. during summer months and until 5:00 p.m. in winter. A map will be provided at the gate. Entrance fee is 75¢ per car. Hikers are admitted free.

PATH OF HISTORY

Monterey's "Path of History" is a well-marked, self-guided, three-mile tour of 45 historic buildings, including the Custom House, Colton Hall, Robert Louis Stevenson House, California's First Theatre, the Old Whaling Station and other sites rich in the area's history. Some have curators on duty and are open to the public; others are private offices and homes. A few of the historic buildings require small entrance fees. Free maps are available at the Monterey History and Art Association, 550 Calle Principal, at Custom House Plaza, and at the Monterey Peninsula Chamber of Commerce office. Allow at least two hours if walking and 1½ hours if driving. Follow the red-orange line.

WALKING TOURS

An enjoyable way to explore Monterey is a walking tour. Four guided tours are offered each day year round:

Tour No. 1—10:00 a.m.—Robert Louis Stevenson House area
Tour No. 2—11:00 a.m.—Custom House Plaza area
Tour No. 3—1:30 p.m.—Monterey Town House and
　　　　　　　　　　　　Old Jail area
Tour No. 4—3:00 p.m.—Cannery Row

The average tour lasts 1½ to 2 hours. Admission fees per tour are: Adults, $2.00; young adults, $1.00; children under twelve, free. This includes entrance fees to historic buildings where required. Individually guided tours anywhere on the Monterey Peninsula are also available at $5.00 per hour. Reservations are required. The California Heritage Guide office is at 181 Pacific Street, Monterey; telephone 373-6454.

BUS AND LIMOUSINE TOURS

Gray Line of Monterey-Carmel at the Southern Pacific Depot, Monterey, has a tour of Monterey and Carmel, 25 miles, about 2½ hours, including Monterey's historic adobes, Cannery Row, Pacific Grove's shoreline, Seventeen Mile Drive, Carmel and Carmel Mission Basilica. This tour leaves at 2:00 p.m. daily during July and August, and Monday, Wednesday, Friday and Saturday during June and September. Fares: Adults, $3.25; under twelve years, $2.00. You may take the same tour in a chauffeured Lincoln Continental for $30.00. Reservations are required; telephone 373-4989. Gray Line also has a tour from Monterey to Hearst Castle at San Simeon June through September.

Chartered Limousine Service, Inc. offers chauffeur-driven sightseeing tours, including after-dark night life tours. Call 394-6519 for information.

Joe's Taxi at Junipero and 4th Avenue, Carmel, provides guided scenic tours of Seventeen Mile Drive and historic points of interest for small parties. For information, call 624-3885.

Escortours will take you to the best restaurants and outstanding events on the Monterey Peninsula. Groups have a minimum of four and no more than six persons, with one well-trained knowledgeable escort. For information concerning these tours, which are more costly since they include transportation, meals and drinks, call 624-3411.

Informal Tours by Norbert Kammer (phone 372-0854) are

available daily or weekly. Emphasis is on a personalized view of the Monterey Peninsula planned around the visitor's interests. Knowledgeable guides plan excursions to make the best use of the time you have available. Fees are reasonable.

BOAT EXCURSIONS

Sam's Fishing Fleet and Frank's Fishing Trips, both at Fisherman's Wharf, have narrated sightseeing cruises around Monterey Bay every day. The cruise lasts 45 minutes. Departures are frequent, and reservations are not necessary. Fares: Adults, $1.50; ages 6-12, $.75; under 6, free. This is one of the best family fun bargains.

12 EXTRASPECIAL EVENTS ON THE MONTEREY PENINSULA

JANUARY

Bing Crosby National Pro-Amateur Golf Championship Tournament, four days—Pebble Beach

Monterey Peninsula Chamber Music Society Concert Series—Sunset Center, Carmel

Monterey County Symphony Association Concert Series

Championship Cat Show, two days—Monterey Fairgrounds

Marina Day—Marina

FEBRUARY

Monterey County Painting Competition—Monterey Peninsula Museum of Art, Monterey

Carmel Music Society Concert Series—Sunset Center, Carmel

MARCH

Rugby Tournament, two days—Collins Field—Pebble Beach

Kar Kapades, three days—Monterey Fairgrounds

Ano Nuevo Race—Monterey Peninsula Yacht Club, Monterey

APRIL

Victorian House Tour, two days—Pacific Grove

Polo Matches—Collins Field, Pebble Beach

Steeplechase—Pebble Beach Equestrian Center

Kite Flying Contest—Carmel High School

Kids' Day—Los Arboles School, Marina

Spring Dressage Competition—Pebble Beach Equestrian Center

Wild Flower Show, three days—Pacific Grove Museum of Natural History

Adobe House Tour, two days—Monterey

MAY

Sports Car Races, three days—Laguna Seca Track, Monterey
Monterey Peninsula Choral Society Concert Series
Home Show, five days—Monterey Fairgrounds
Bonsai Show, two days—Monterey Peninsula Buddhist Temple, Seaside
Pony Club Horse Show—Pebble Beach Equestrian Center
Commodore's Regatta—Stillwater Cove, Pebble Beach
Del Monte Dog Show, two days—Collins Field, Pebble Beach
Garden Tour—Monterey Peninsula Volunteer Services
Lesler Memorial Race—Monterey Peninsula Yacht Club, Monterey
Moss Landing Marine Laboratories Open House—Moss Landing
Shark Derby—Moss Landing

JUNE

Shark Derby—Moss Landing
Merienda, Monterey's Birthday Celebration—Memory Garden, Monterey
Arts and Crafts Festival, two days—Custom House Plaza, Monterey
Sports Car Races, three days—Laguna Seca Track, Monterey
Morgan Horse Show, three days—Monterey Fairgrounds

JULY

Santanorama—Stillwater Cove, Pebble Beach
Matthew C. Jenkins Mercury Series—Stillwater Cove, Pebble Beach
Fourth of July Parade—Seaside
Sloat Landing Re-Enactment—Custom House Plaza, Monterey
Evening Fireworks Display—Monterey Municipal Beach

120

Clint Eastwood Invitational Celebrity Tennis Tournament, three days—Pebble Beach

Obon Festival, two days—Monterey Fairgrounds

Antique Show and Sale, three days—Monterey Fairgrounds

Arts and Crafts Festival, two days—Custom House Plaza, Monterey

Arabian Horse Show, three days—Monterey Fairgrounds

Bach Festival, fourteen days—Sunset Center, Carmel

Highland Games—Collins Field, Pebble Beach

Feast of Lanterns, four days—Pacific Grove

Feast of Lanterns Yacht Race—Monterey Peninsula Yacht Club, Monterey

Soap Box Derby—Laguna Seca Track, Monterey

Espiritu Santos Portuguese Festival, two days—Portuguese Hall, Monterey

Equestrian Event for Western American Perpetual Cups, three days—Pebble Beach Equestrian Center

Motorcycle Races, two days—Laguna Seca Track, Monterey

AUGUST

Gwen Graham Concours d'Elegance—Del Monte Lodge, Pebble Beach

National Horse Show, five days—Monterey Fairgrounds

Monterey County Fair, five days—Monterey Fairgrounds

Arts and Crafts Festival, two days—Custom House Plaza, Monterey

Dressage Championship—Pebble Beach Equestrian Center

Summer Horse Show, four days—Pebble Beach Equestrian Center

Beach and Tennis Club Championship—Beach and Tennis Club Courts, Pebble Beach

Annual Festival and Fish Fry, two days—Moss Landing

121

SEPTEMBER

Equestrian Trials, three days—Pebble Beach Equestrian Center

Labor Day Mercury Regatta—Stillwater Cove, Pebble Beach

Monterey Jazz Festival, three days—Monterey Fairgrounds

Festival of the Parade of Nations, two days—Custom House Plaza, Monterey

House Tour—Women's Architectural League

S.F.B. Morse Regatta—Stillwater Cove, Pebble Beach

Gem and Mineral Show, two days—Monterey Fairgrounds

Water Color Show—Pacific Grove Museum of Natural History

Santa Rosalia Blessing of the Fleet—Fisherman's Wharf, Monterey

Artichoke Festival, three days—Castroville

OCTOBER

Social Spectator Polo, three days—Collins Field, Pebble Beach

Sports Car Races, three days—Laguna Seca Track, Monterey

Sand Castle Contest—Carmel Beach

Hole-in-One Contest—Pacific Grove Golf Links

Butterfly Parade—Pacific Grove

Paisano El Toro Race—Monterey Peninsula Yacht Club, Monterey

Pumpkin-Carving Contest—Del Monte Hyatt House, Monterey

Hallowe'en Parade and Party—Moss Landing

NOVEMBER

Homecrafters' Marketplace—Sunset Center, Carmel

Golden Domino Tournament—Del Monte Lodge, Pebble Beach

Backgammon Tournament—Del Monte Lodge, Pebble Beach

Competitive Art Exhibition—Seaside City Hall

Community Thanksgiving Potluck Dinner—Monterey Fairgrounds

122

DECEMBER

Festival of the Trees, three days—Monterey Peninsula Museum of Art, Monterey

39 Craftsmen Bring Christmas, three days—La Playa Hotel, Carmel

Santa Claus Parade—Pacific Grove

Filipino Maria Clara Festival—Monterey Fairgrounds

Singing Christmas Tree—Assembly of God Church, Pacific Grove

Residential Christmas Tour—Pacific Grove

INDEX

125

$1.95 EACH—WESTERN TRAVEL BOOKS FROM WARD RITCHIE PRESS

Trips for the Day, Week-end or Longer

ALL BOOKS COMPLETE, MANY WITH PHOTOGRAPHS AND MAPS

QUANTITY		TOTAL
☐	**BACKYARD TREASURE HUNTING**	$ _____
☐	**BAJA CALIFORNIA:** Vanished Missions, Lost Treasures, Strange Stories True and Tall	$ _____
☐	**BICYCLE TOURING IN LOS ANGELES**	$ _____
☐	**EXPLORING BIG SUR, CARMEL AND MONTEREY**	$ _____
☐	**EXPLORING CALIFORNIA BYWAYS, #1** From Kings Canyon to the Mexican Border	$ _____
☐	**EXPLORING CALIFORNIA BYWAYS, #2** In and Around Los Angeles	$ _____
☐	**EXPLORING CALIFORNIA BYWAYS, #3** Desert Country	$ _____
☐	**EXPLORING CALIFORNIA BYWAYS, #4** Mountain Country	$ _____
☐	**EXPLORING CALIFORNIA BYWAYS, #5** Historic Sites of California	$ _____
☐	**EXPLORING CALIFORNIA BYWAYS, #6** Owens Valley	$ _____
☐	**EXPLORING CALIFORNIA BYWAYS, #7** An Historical Sketchbook	$ _____
☐	**EXPLORING CALIFORNIA FOLKLORE**	$ _____
☐	**EXPLORING THE SANTA BARBARA COUNTRY**	$ _____
☐	**EXPLORING SMALL TOWNS, No. 1**	$ _____
☐	**GREAT BIKE TOURS IN NORTHERN CALIFORNIA**	$ _____
☐	**GUIDEBOOK TO THE DELTA COUNTRY OF CENTRAL CALIFORNIA**	$ _____
☐	**GUIDEBOOK TO THE COLORADO DESERT OF CALIFORNIA**	$ _____
☐	**GUIDEBOOK TO THE FEATHER RIVER COUNTRY**	$ _____
☐	**GUIDEBOOK TO THE LAKE TAHOE COUNTRY, VOL. I.** Echo Summit, Squaw Valley and the California Shore	$ _____
☐	**GUIDEBOOK TO THE LAKE TAHOE COUNTRY, VOL. II.** Alpine County, Donner-Truckee, and the Nevada Shore	$ _____
☐	**GUIDEBOOK TO LAS VEGAS**	$ _____
☐	**GUIDEBOOK TO THE MOJAVE DESERT OF CALIFORNIA,** Including Death Valley, Joshua Tree National Monument, and the Antelope Valley	$ _____

[SEE MORE BOOKS AND ORDER FORM ON OTHER SIDE]